Missionary you

God Bless You,

Alive Again!

Bishop T. T. Kelly

This sickness is not unto death, but for the glory of God,
that the Son of God might be glorified thereby.
—John 11:4

Alive Again!

My Story: A Miraculous Memoir

Bishop Lorenzo L. Kelly

To order additional copies of this book, contact:
Xlibris Corporation
1-888-795-4274
www.Xlibris.com
Orders@Xlibris.com
74956

CONTENTS

Acknowledgments

Thank you to my wife, Evelyn. Appreciations to my eldest son who is no longer with us, Thomas Kelly; my sons, Scott Fitzerald and Loren Everett and their families; my brother, Chuck L. Kelly; my sisters, Barbara Kelly-Gilbert and Neva Brown; my wife's brother and sister, Jim Heard and Grace Martinez.

Additionally, there were so many people who were instrumental in both the hospitalization and in the recovery processes until it's hard to remember everyone. However, I would be remiss in not mentioning the following people, some of whom are mentioned in the book and others who are not. Elder and Mrs. Lawrence Cliette, Deacon Harold Thompson, Minister Elston Dacus, Sister Franceen Robinson, Sister Leonne Seevers, Sister Linda Ault, Sister Leona Derden, Elder Troy Carr, Evangelist Twana Carr, Attorney Al Scovel, Judge Janine Kern, Judge Marshall Young, Judge Merton Tice, Sister Trivia Afraid of Lightning, Judge Jack Delaney, Sister Maggie Morrison, Brother Bill Burnette, Sister Kim Ault, Missionary Denise Crayton, Dr. Tom and Ruth Udager, Elder Herman Hicks, Brother Matthew Mock, Elder Ezzard Luke, Pastor and Mrs. James Henderson, and Cliff and Georgia Melrose.

Foreword

I had not been in a church for at least six years because I had become disillusioned with organized religion. The duplicity of it all was more than I could take. Saving the saved and feeding the fed didn't do it for me anymore. Then one Sunday I found myself in one of the oldest church buildings in town. Bishop Kelly stood at the pulpit elegant in his vestments, preaching to a multi-racial congregation and fifteen or so inmates from our local jail. He spoke about pain and the hope of redemption through faith in Christ. Bishop Kelly asked those with infirmities to come forward for healing. This was a surprise to me as I had never seen anything like it before. He looked from person to person and stopped and said to me "your hips have been hurting for a long time—if you want to be healed, come forward". What choice did I have—I went forward and was miraculously healed. If you experience healing, you believe.

Over the next few years I saw healings of body, mind and spirit. I also learned that this black man had served three days a week gratuitously and consistently for over a decade as chaplain of our local jail. My affection and admiration for him deepened over the years as I witnessed the real changes he made in people's lives.

Recently, late one afternoon, I received a call. Bishop Kelly had been taken to the hospital suffering from a thoracic aortic aneurysm. Eighteen inches of his aorta was replaced in a ten hour operation. During the first operation and the following days of recovery he died and was brought back a number of times. The surgeon told us only one out of ten makes it through the operation and recovery would be fraught with complications. Bishop's legs had also been burned during the operation necessitating two full rounds of skin grafting. Within forty-five days Bishop left the hospital. Indeed God answered our prayers with a miracle—full recovery! Within two more weeks Bishop Kelly once again stood at the pulpit, elegant in his vestments, yes, but a wiser, more eloquent man. This was a man who had experienced, literally, the presence and counsel of Christ. He told us he was a dead man and returned. He said "I have been to a place I have never been before. I have seen things I've never seen before. I've seen heaven and I've seen hell. Heaven is a place so wonderful, you can not realize how really wonderful it is and "yes" there is peace. Hell is a place you don't want to go. I heard screaming and crying and witnessed anguish." He went on to say that holding on to regrets, resentments, grudges and old hurts is a waste of time and energy. "All it does is separate you from the Lord." He advised to always extend forgiveness and love and be determined to serve the Lord. His message is full of hope, conviction and love. He continues to be an inspiration and the Lord's spokesman to all. He speaks of the Christ and His compassion—Christ's wonderful voice filled with kindness and love. He continues to serve as an example to all through God the Father, God the Son and God the Holy Spirit.

It is my experience that Bishop Kelly is a man of God fittingly endowed with dignity, graciousness, knowledge and discretion. He continues to fight generously for the cause of God. When his sight and breathing failed, his disembodied soul saw the marvels and holy light of heaven and the terror and torture of hell. This experience has made Bishop Kelly just as strong as gentle, beaming with brightness and affection, hope and peace, reverence and sympathy. A Catholic bishop and good friend, Bishop Cupich said while praying to God for Bishop Kelly's healing, "Lord, restore Bishop Kelly to his full function. We need him here with us more than you need him there."

Bishop Kelly's unique experience has been shared with tens of thousands of people enabling them to connect and appreciate the life hereafter that awaits us all, because God has willed it so. Let us take courage for our eternal welfare.

Allen Scovel, Attorney
Rapid City, South Dakota

About the Pastor

Bishop Lorenzo Lee Kelly was born in Winter Park, Florida in 1943. The family moved to Evanston, Illinois, in 1955, where he attended Haven Junior High School and Evanston Township High School, graduating in June 1961. He worked one year and attended Loop Junior College the next year. In August 1963, he had the honor of being the first black male to be hired in a North Shore Bank during those heated times of civil unrest of the '60s. As his job became a career, he worked his way up within the bank being promoted as he went and while pursuing higher education through the American Banking Association. He started in the proof department, worked as a teller for a number of years before serving as customer service staff, assistant cashier, personal banking officer, and finally, as assistant vice president and drive-in bank manager. God gave him favor within the bank and without, in the Evanston and surrounding community.

As a young boy in Florida, his family had been members of Bethel Missionary Baptist Church in Winter Park. In Evanston, they became members of the Springfield Missionary Baptist Church. This is where Kelly met his bride-to-be, Evelyn Ann Heard, and where both of their families were members. On October 10, 1964, he and his fiancé Evelyn A. Heard were wed at the Springfield Baptist Church in a beautiful ceremony, attended by a standing-room-only crowd of friends and family from the churches and the community. To the union of Lorenzo L. and Evelyn A. Kelly was born three beautiful sons—Thomas, Scott, and Loren. They are blessed to have two daughters of marriage. Shelly is married to Scott, and they have three awesome daughters—Mikaela, Aleah, and Jahnaya—and Cara is married to Loren, and they have two beautiful daughters, Beatriz and Grace. The Kellys are blessed to have many, many other children whom they love as though they were born to them.

In 1969, Kelly moved his church membership from Springfield Baptist to Faith Temple Church of God in Christ, also in Evanston, Illinois, where the pastor is Bishop Carlis L. Moody Sr. In 1973, Kelly, under the leadership, teaching, and tutelage of Bishop Moody, acknowledged the Lord's call upon his life as a minister of the Gospel. Kelly became a licensed minister on January 20, 1974, and immediately began attending the Moody Bible Institute's Evening School Division in Chicago, Illinois (this school is not associated with Bishop Carlis Moody). Graduating in May 1978, he continued to serve in the ministry of Faith Temple Church of God in Christ in Evanston. He was ordained as an elder on August 25, 1979, by the late Bishop Louis Henry Ford. In August 1982, the Kellys were led by the Lord to move to Rapid City, South Dakota, to begin their ministry. He left the bank management position at First Bank of Evanston, after nineteen years, and she left her office manager position at College Entrance Examination Board's midwestern division after four years. The new church, which they founded in Rapid City, was named after their home church in Evanston, Illinois, Faith Temple Church of God in Christ.

On November 12, 1990, Kelly was promoted to the office of Bishop—from being an ordained elder to the bishop of the state of South Dakota for the Church of God in Christ (appointed by the late Bishop Louis Henry Ford, the appointment was ratified by the 1990 General Assembly). He was officially consecrated to the office of Bishop on May 30, 1991, in Rapid City at a service officiated by the late Bishop Ford. As a bishop, he is one of approximately 175 other Church of God in Christ bishops and is a member of the COGIC Board of Bishops. Bishop Kelly is frequently invited as a guest evangelist/preacher to churches all across America, as well as to foreign countries.

He served as jail chaplain and has ministered to inmates at the Pennington County Jail, as well as state prison inmates for more than fifteen years. In addition, he served on the Pennington County Jail Advisory Board for over twenty years. Over the years, he taught a weekly life-changing class entitled "Maximized Manhood" for the male inmates with up to thirty men attending weekly. There was always a long waiting list of those desiring to attend. He writes and visits prisoners throughout South Dakota and the surrounding states as a follow-up to those from the jail. He retired at the end of December 2006 from his regular involvement with the jail. Because of his work in the Rapid City community, Bishop Kelly received the South Dakota Education Association's Human and Civil

Rights award in 1995. In May of 2002, he received the Liberty Bell Award from the Pennington County Bar Association for his work with jail and prison inmates. In May of 2006, he received the I Believe in Kids award from Wellspring Inc. In January of 2007, he received the first King Spirit Award for unity in diversity from the Spiritual Assembly of the Baha'is of Rapid City.

Bishop Lorenzo L. Kelly is quite a *miracle* as he is the survivor of an aneurysm of the thoracic aorta, which he suffered and underwent emergency surgery for replacement of eighteen inches of his aorta on January 28, 2006. Medically speaking, only 10 percent of people are blessed to get off the operating table, but then to be able to go on and live a good, healthy life is rare. He died approximately five times during the surgery and had other severe complications including accidentally receiving fourth-degree burns to the front of both legs. He had a number of surgeries, had to be shocked back to life a number of times, while he lay critically ill several weeks, and later, had additional skin graft operations to repair the damaged legs. During hospitalization, he sustained the hospital Staph infection, which has killed hundreds of people, but thank God, he lived. He also had an *E. coli* infection in his left kneecap, twice between the skin-graft surgeries. It's been a long suffering way over the past year, but God's grace and mercy have proven to be enough to bring this great man of God through to complete recovery.

Faith Temple Church will be celebrating its twenty-eighth church anniversary along with the twentieth jurisdictional anniversary in late July of 2010. We're hoping the community will come and be a part of the celebration and rejoicing along with us as we have a lot to rejoice about!

Prelude

in medias res

Satan's Death Wish for My Life—BUT GOD!

Just over four years ago, on January 28, 2006, at nine o'clock in the morning, I suffered an aneurysm of the thoracic aorta. It was such a severe pain that was ripping through my body from the upper chest down into the lower stomach and around into my lower back. Immediately, I realized that I was at the point of death and began to say to my wife, "Honey, I love you!" and to the Lord, "Lord, You know I love You!" and breaking forth from my mouth was a most unusual language. The Holy Ghost began an urgent discourse in an "unknown language." Words, I'm sure that were pleading for my life before the throne of God.

This dialogue in the above order continued the entire time that my wife and I waited for the ambulance to arrive since she had immediately called 911 when I alerted her of the intense pain that had just started in my chest. I could have and would have died right there in my bedroom had it not been for the power and pleading of the Holy Ghost as my life hung in the balance. The surgeon later explained that this actually should have been a massive brain stroke, but instead of traveling up into my head, it ripped the inner lining of the aorta from the top, where the valve connects the aorta to the heart, downward all the way to just above my renal arteries. As I rode in the ambulance, the Holy Ghost continued to speak through me in intense prayer as I was still in intense pain.

During the ten hours of surgery, eighteen inches of my aorta was replaced, and the surgical team worked feverishly to save my life. Even so, I died five times on the operating table. In order to ensure the possibility of a successful operation, after being rushed into emergency surgery:

- my body was frozen down to thirty-six degrees;
- I was revived from death five times;
- my body temperature plummeted down to a freezing fifteen to eighteen degrees;
- attempts to warm body were failing, and heat was placed around my body;
- I received, accidentally, severe fourth-degree burns to the front of both legs;
- because of the burns and to help avoid infection, I was pumped full of fluids;
- I received more than thirty-seven units of blood and blood products (three times my body usage);
- my body became extensively swollen due to the fluids, and my chest had to remain open, wrapped in cellophane-like material, for the next three days.
- twenty-four-hour dialysis was performed to pull off the excess water in hopes of closing the surgery site as soon as possible;
- my body was kept in an induced comatose state and on complete life support for several days;
- four hours after leaving surgery, I was rushed back into surgery to locate and stop unknown bleeding in the chest. I was in the second surgery for six hours. THIS WAS WHEN THEY SAID, "If you want to see him alive, come now!"
- Finally, they located and stopped the bleeding though the doctors could not guarantee that I would not start bleeding again. NOR COULD THEY SAY WHETHER I WOULD LIVE OR DIE. They did say that ONLY ONE OUT OF TEN people get off the operating table alive and that I WAS IN THE 10 PERCENT!
- on the afternoon of the next day, January 29, was returned to surgery to debride (pronounced de-breed) the burn wounds on my legs. This was the first of many surgeries to the burn sites;
- on January 31, I was returned to surgery for debridement of the burns and closing of the sternum;

- I went into a code-blue situation after being returned to my room and was shocked multiple times to bring me back;
- over the next two weeks, I had multiple operations to the chest and back where tubes had to be inserted to drain off infections that were lodging in my body.
- I REMAINED in critical condition in surgical intensive care for two and a half weeks;
- during this time, I sustained the hospital-borne Staph infection that has claimed the lives of more than eighteen thousand (according to 2005 data) and which, approximately, ninety thousand people in America had contracted;
- I became a dialysis patient. I died twice while in the process of receiving dialysis, and both times, I had out-of-body death experiences.
- during surgery and while frozen, I sustained strokes in both eyes due to the lack of blood supply during that time. As a result, my vision was impaired, and I could not see clearly;
- due to the extended time having the breathing tube down my throat, I received damage to my vocal cord and could not speak above a whisper;
- I was not able to eat for weeks and lost more than fifty pounds;
- I could not walk due to the extensive burns and resulting reoccurring surgeries.

I was in the hospital for a total of six weeks going from surgical intensive care to medical intensive care to pulmonary care to the Rehabilitation Institute and was discharged March 15, 2006. Sometime during all of this, I had skin grafts performed to both legs, and they took donor skin from around my thighs. By this time, all of my body functions had returned, and where there had been a question as to whether I would be a lifetime dialysis patient, my kidneys began to function normally. I returned to the hospital on March 31 for two more weeks—more surgery (a second skin graft, which did take this time) to the burn sites and returned home in mid-April. The second skin graft required them to take donor skin from my thighs, between the first strips taken, as well as from my hips. Still healing in the back and chest surgery sites, now I was bloody and raw from my waist down to midlegs near the ankles. While in the hospital and after being discharged, I needed extensive help from family and home health nursing staff and could not care for myself.

On two occasions, (Easter Sunday and Mother's Day Sunday) I sustained the *E. coli* infection to the left knee area of the burn surgical site. The last time was on Mother's Day, and I had to, literally, be carried home from the church service. I was in so much pain I could not bear to place weight on the left leg. I was given over the phone medical advice and had to endure the most excruciating pain for the rest of that day and all day Monday. The doctor, on Monday evening, sent me from his office straight to the hospital's emergency room where they diagnosed the *E. coli* infection and, this time, instead of antibiotics, they would need to perform a surgical washing to remove the infection. I reentered the hospital on Tuesday morning, May 16, had surgery that afternoon where they put holes in the kneecap to enable the infection to be washed out and thereby removed them from my body. I was discharged from the hospital on May 18, 2006.

The Lord has blessed me to be almost completely restored at this time. I can see, walk, talk, sing, and praise the Lord. All of my normal bodily functions returned, and I am not a patient of any kind. I've been released by the physicians, and they are pleased to call me the miracle! As well, I am pleased to be God's miracle!

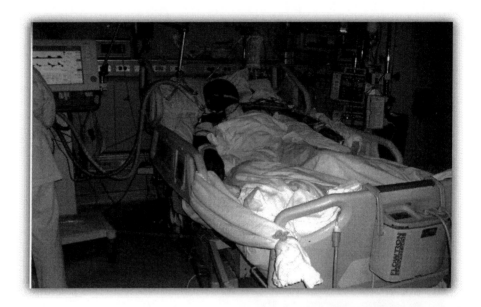

↑ PHOTO ABOVE: Bishop Lorenzo L. Kelly critically ill and on the ventilator for life support from an aneurysm of the thoracic aorta and other complications including fourth-degree burns to the front of both legs. (January 2006)

PHOTO: Bishop Lorenzo L. Kelly, → nearly four years later celebrating his forty-fifth wedding anniversary in Kauai, Hawaii. (October 2009)

THE LORD is my shepherd; I shall not want.
He maketh me to lie down in green pastures:
he leadeth me beside the still waters.
He restoreth my soul: he leadeth me in the
path of righteousness for his name's sake.
Yea, though I walk through the valley of the
shadow of death, I will fear no evil:
for thou art with me; thy rod and thy
staff they comfort me.
Thou preparest a table before me
in the presence of mine enemies:
thou anointest my head with oil;
my cup runneth over.
Surely goodness and mercy shall follow me
all the days of my life: and I will dwell in the
house of the LORD forever.
—Psalms 23

Chapter 1

I SHALL NOT DIE BUT LIVE!

Dialysis was being performed on me in my intensive care room, a unit was brought in since I could not be moved at that time. I remember seeing a nurse I knew who had taken care of my mother, when she was a dialysis patient, several years earlier. Of course, I didn't realize that I was on dialysis, I was just glad to see Joy. I was partially out of sorts and didn't know what had happened or was happening to me. I had written a note asking my wife, "Is that Joy?" She didn't know the lady's name and was not sure of what I was asking her. Suddenly, I remember spinning out of control and remembering that it had happened to me one other time when I had ended up in heaven. So I made a circular motion to my wife, just above my chest area, to say that I felt my spirit leaving my body. I left the hospital room and flew into outer space. The weightless feeling as I flew was wonderful, and I was so happy to be going back to heaven to be with the Lord! I wanted to go as I noticed the blackness of outer space with the beautiful sparkling stars. Then I heard my wife calling me. She said, "Lorenzo, don't you leave, come back in the name of Jesus!" Then she began to quote Psalms 118:17, **"I shall not die, but live, and declare the works of the LORD."**

As I began to repeat those words after her, I found myself back in the room hanging in the ceiling, watching the medical staff working on me. I had no way of knowing that my sister Neva was visiting me, and this was my first time seeing her as she was standing there at the foot of my bed. I thought she was praying. Evelyn was on the side of my bed, speaking the Word of God into me and calling me back to life. As I slowly, inaudibly mouthed the scripture, repeating her words, I reentered my body, feeling the pain of reentry and shock of electricity. It was months later before Evelyn and I actually talked about this event, and that was when she confirmed to me that Neva *was* there in that intensive care room on that day, and she, further, explained to me exactly what Neva was doing. You've got to know her, but I'll explain here that my baby sister, Neva Brown, is simply a radical for the Lord. The way Evelyn tells it, Neva surely went radical that day and began to speak in a most violent way to Satan as she demanded that he take his hands off of her brother. She was speaking in a low, growly type of voice as she spoke in other tongues. When she did speak in

A summary of Bishop Kelly's accounts of his times with the LORD as he was led by Jesus past walls of flames of fire which he recognized to be hell. He heard voices shouting "It's not Buddha, it's not Mohammed, it's not Allah, IT'S JESUS! JESUS! JESUS!" In Heaven, he visited a place where there seemed to be millions of aborted babies, strewn across a lawn appearing like small bushes, there was so many of those precious babies, there was not enough room and a new building was being built near an older building that housed the children. Bishop Kelly recounts seeing his mother and Evelyn's mother and asking Jesus to let him remain there with them to help but was motioned on and heard Jesus' sweet voice say…

"Come with me, you've always wanted to help!" He desired to remain in heaven but then he says, "I heard my wife's sweet voice calling me back!" and I recall the pain of my soul reentering my body. "I desired to remain in Heaven, but I'm glad to be back here with you!" WELL, "I'm glad, too, Honey!"

English, Evelyn heard her saying things like "No, you don't Satan! The blood of Jesus! Take your hands off of my brother!"

That last experience with dying, when Evelyn called me back, I experienced the power of the Word and the power of the love a wife can have for her husband. I heard my wife's sweet voice calling me back! And I recall the pain of my soul reentering my body. I heard the love in her voice as she called to me and now I have an even greater understanding of the meaning of one flesh. I heard the love in her voice as she called me. I have an even greater understanding of the meaning of what *one flesh* means.

"Therefore shall a man leave his father and his mother, and shall cleave unto his wife: and they shall be one flesh"—Gen. 2:24. So, I ask you this question—who has more power over *my body* but the other part of me? *We are one flesh!* Please don't ask me how I could be sailing past the stars and yet hear Evelyn calling me by my name. I don't know—but I did!

I say that it was the next day, but I really don't know. I just remember seeing and thanking the doctor for having worked so hard to save my life. Dr. Gordon by now was calling me his miracle. He said that we both know that he did not do anything but that "It was the Man upstairs." I am known to be quick-witted, and it sprang into action as I quickly asked, "What floor is He on? But if you mean Jesus, I know He did it but thank you for all you did too." Later that morning, another doctor came into my room and talked with me. When I mentioned being "a miracle," he said, "I wouldn't go that far!" I retorted that Dr. Gordon said that I was, and when I mentioned the other doctor, he dropped his head and agreed that I was a miracle.

FIRE

"Yea, though I walk through the valley of the shadow of death, I will fear no evil: for thou art with me; thy rod and thy staff they comfort me."

Now, let me tell you about one of the occasions—one of the other times that I died . . . I remember going through darkness, and in the darkness, I heard cursing. I said to the Lord, because He was in the darkness with me, "Oh, I'm sorry, Lord! I've . . . I've learned how to curse again!" I said, "I don't talk that way, and I don't know where that came from but please forgive me for speaking like that!" Well, we continued on through this darkness, and I don't know where it was, but I know that I was with Him and that he was taking me to another place." We stepped out of the darkness and to my left there was burning fire! Immediately, I heard people crying, and as they cried, I heard some of them screaming and saying, "It's not Buddha! It's not Muhammad! It's not Allah! IT'S JESUS! JESUS! JESUS!" As they screamed and cried, I wanted to step a little closer just to see who was in that boiling hot place. I had the understanding, at that moment, that this hell was full of people and even some who had seemingly lived for the Lord. I further understood that it was too late for them and that they were inside of their destiny.

The man that was leading me, THE LORD, motioned to me, and we began to climb. I was reminded of the song, "How I Got Over." "My soul looks back and wonder how I got over." Part of the chorus says, "Move on up a little higher." And I just kept moving on up a little higher—going still higher and then . . . eventually! I looked to my left, and there was my mother and my mother-in-law standing side by side with their backs turned to me, but I recognized them. They were doing what they most loved to do in this life, both of them were eating. I recognized the size of their hips and began to laugh—laughing for joy! As I laughed, they turned around and looked at me with smiles on their faces but no words. I was so delighted that I had found my two moms. I started to run toward my mother, wanting to tell her how much I loved her, missed her and how glad I was to see her. I needed to tell her that Evelyn and I had done our best trying to take care of her while she lived with us and during her sickness. I was so glad to see both of my moms, and I asked the person guiding me, "Can I stay here with them?" He didn't say anything to me but motioned again for me to come with him.

HIGHER

They never motioned for me to come to them. I started walking with Him, following Him, again as we moved on up a little higher. We came to a place near where my moms were, and at first glance, there appeared to be bushes all over the yard. A whole lot of bushes! Well, when I looked again, I realized that what appeared as bushes were actually little babies. I was given the understanding that these were aborted babies, and I was so amazed. I had the understanding that my moms were helping to take care of those aborted babies and that some of those babies were from our own families (secrets). They were in front of an old building, and we went inside and rested. I believe that God is angry with America for the babies that they have killed through abortion. He's called the whole world into account for their deeds—but America! America is . . . is the land that was founded because people were seeking religious freedom. Now, our nation has backslidden so much until even the churches have blasphemed against Him and all the standards of holiness are gone. We're after members, money but not souls. God, forgive us!

The next morning when we got up, I came out of that old building, and next door to it was a building that people were working on. They were building it for these new babies because there wasn't enough room for them. I asked if I could stay there and help and I heard laughter like I've never heard before, MY LORD! It was so overwhelming . . . laughter that filled every space! Oh, and peace that was everywhere! My, my! I feel God's presence every time I start talking about it!

He said, "No, you can't—come with me! You've been helping people your whole life—you come with me!" When I heard *that* laughter, I realized that I was in the very presence of the LORD JESUS CHRIST. I exclaimed, "Oh my god! I've been walking with Jesus!"

"I come to the garden alone while the dew is still on the roses. And the voice I hear, falling on my ear, the son of God . . ." Bless His name! Walking with the KING OF KINGS and the LORD OF LORDS! I took off running and hurrying up to catch up with him as we continued to go up a little higher. The beauty of that place—the colors, the brightness—is simply indescribable! Suddenly, I was back in my hospital bed, but I had been with Jesus. Oh, I've heard Him! No hallucinations! NO! I AM NOT OUT OF MY MIND. I've been with the LORD! I praise Him for that!

DELIVERANCE

Faith Temple Church of God in Christ in Evanston, Illinois, is where the Lord delivered my soul and where, as we say, "I was reclaimed—Praise God!" I had been living in sin—a condition that was not conducive to the call that God had upon my life from birth! Satan decided that he'd better destroy me while he had me in his horrible clutches and when I realized anything, I was running back to the Lord. I was terrified and desperate. I didn't even know if the Lord would accept me back into the fold after

the things that I had done and had been involved in. Nevertheless, I came running and made it in through the doors of that wonderful church sanctuary. The pastor, Bishop Carlis L. Moody Sr., great man of God that he is, received me and spiritually nurtured me as one of the sheep of the fold. Thank God there was a place of refuge for me—a place of safety and growth. That was in the late 1960s, and I've lived for the Lord since that time. It

About a month before the aneurysm was through the teaching and preaching of the Gospel that I was able to make it. Bishop Moody put the Word of God out before his congregation as meticulously as if he was preparing a great meal—Sunday morning and evening services; Tuesday and Friday evening services—he put the word out and I ate it! Like it says in the book of Jeremiah **"Thy words were found, and I did eat them; and thy word was unto me the joy and rejoicing of mine heart, for I am called by thy name, O LORD God of hosts"**—Jeremiah 15:16. I was a starving man, spiritually, and had been strengthened and nourished in all the things of the Lord. When it came time that the Lord would send us out, into the wilderness, to start our own ministry. What name was it that I would choose for the Rapid City church but Faith Temple Church of God in Christ? I had been taught the word, and little did I know that God was truly going to establish faith in me.

Many times, my wife and I didn't know how we were going to pay ours or the churches bills. For a season, it seemed as if we were all alone and that there was no one who cared about us—no one inquired as to our well-being. We really only heard from the Church of God in Christ when there were financial reports due. No one ever called just to say "How are you doing?" Yet, in the midst of the seeming neglect, God always delivered us. Praise God! Sometimes, it might be in the ninth hour, the tenth hour or later. Sometimes, just when we were most desperate and most vulnerable enough to give up—that's when the Lord would step in and handle the situation. So many times, just when we were so desperate, didn't know what to do, and gave up—don't know why it's like that—but that's when He would show up. Evelyn and I both believed that God wanted to get the glory and that He wanted to be our answer. Bishop Moody always sings the song, "Christ is the Answer" and, truly God has shown us that He not only hears us but He also attends to our every cry. He has, indeed, become our **answer** in *every* situation! **"It is good for me that I have been afflicted; that I might learn thy statutes"**—Ps. 119:71. We were able to learn to have trust and faith in the Lord which has brought us through any difficult situations.

FAITH

Especially because of these experiences, I've always considered myself a man of faith to just believe God, and no matter how long it would take, he would always answer! Praise God! However, when I was going through the tremendous suffering because of the burns—months of it—it was hard to continue on in faith. So much pain, so much suffering, and some mistreatment by the hospital staff. I couldn't tell when or how the Lord would answer me. I knew He had to! In a thousand years, I never would have imagined the suffering that I was to go through. I've always believed that I am a man of faith, and being a man of faith, I . . . I know the Word in Psalm 34:19 says, "Many are the afflictions of the righteous: but the LORD delivereth him out of them all." I know that, but I thought perhaps a few days . . . but never like this. I never imagined I would have to really suffer. When you have never been through something like this, you think that whatever it is, "Lord . . . I can do it!" However, when the test comes, many of us find ourselves crying and complaining. Now, I know that there are some who are able to praise their way through their tests but I was not one of those during this time of severe testing.

WHY, LORD?

Since I have tried to live for the Lord and have, indeed, lived for Him most of my life, I wondered why it was taking so long for Him to deliver me from this great trial. While the medical team was concentrating on keeping me alive. I died five times on the operating table during the first ten-hour surgery—another catastrophe occurred. My body had been purposely frozen, my head packed in ice while my head vessels were dissected. I became hypothermic and heat was placed around me to assist in bringing my body temperature back up, quickly. Just imagine, I had the aneurysm of the thoracic aorta—eighteen inches down to just above the renal arteries; was frozen and became hypothermic; was shocked back to life multiple times; had head and chest vessels disconnected and reconnected; and, during this whole process, I sustained severe burns on both of my legs. The burns, at first, seemed inconsequential but later became as big of a problem, or bigger, than the aneurysm. I am scarred from my neck all the way to my feet. It certainly took me into a longer process of healing than I would have gone through if I had not been accidentally roasted while on the operating table.

As mentioned earlier, at first the burns seemed merely superficial like a light sunburn and no one seemed to realize until later the depth of what they were dealing with. There was a process that is called debridement or "debriding" that was required in order to cut down under the burns to below the nerve endings. This debriding process was done several times until the wounds were larger and deeper than at first was known. Ultimately, bone was exposed on the left knee and right tibia or shin. It seemed that no one had seen burns to this depth and these wounds had to be handled in a very careful manner. They required frequent dressing changes with salves, gauzes, and wrappings. The plastic surgeon's nurse said that he had questioned whether or not the legs could be saved. Just thinking about that makes me want to cry because I am fortunate to have legs that I can walk with. They didn't give up—they fought for my legs as hard as they fought to save my life from the aneurysm.

Still, I have questioned God with the big *W* word! I have asked Him, "Why? Why did this happen to me? My sister Barbara said, "Why not you?" And, I respect my older sister but I really wanted to reply to her, laughingly. "Barb, why not *you*?" Oh well! Bless the Lord! I've had so many problems with my legs. That suffering continued throughout three more surgeries where, twice, they cut slices of skin from my hips and thighs to cover the burn sites. Additionally, they split and removed muscle from the back of each leg and used that to cover the areas where my bones were exposed, then they covered that with my own skin harvested from my own body. I was a bloody mess from both hips, both thighs and all the way down to the mid-point of each leg. MY GOD! I almost felt like what Jesus said upon the Cross of Calvary, **"And at the ninth hour Jesus cried with a loud voice, saying, Eloi' Eloi', lama' sabachthani'? which is, being interpreted, My God, my God, why hast thou forsaken me?"**—Mark 15:34. I cried more that year, 2006, than I've, probably, cried in my entire lifetime. I've awakened many nights crying like a baby or trying to tell my wife what was wrong and crying. I just never knew that there were so many tears. Nevertheless, as I look back, I think again, *How did I get over?* My soul looks back and wonders how I got over. Praise God!

Chapter 2

in extremis

VISITORS

For more than two weeks, I was kept in a drug-induced coma, on the Ventilator for life support and gradually I woke up from that long time of being in darkness. My wife told me that during those days, I was still ministering to people in a way. When family and friends were allowed into my surgical intensive care room, if I was awake, I would respond to their visits by blinking or smiling. I said, "I don't know anything about that." She said, "Well, you did." She said that I looked at my children and smiled, especially, when I saw my son, Elder Herman Hicks (from Wichita, Kansas) that I put a big smile on my face and I was so happy to see him. I don't remember seeing him. Praise God! The wonderful thing about the people who love me, they came to see about me from the moment they heard the sad news! They came by car and by airplane but they were here and quickly. Our sons from Minneapolis—Thomas (now deceased), Scott, and Loren; Shelly and Cara; Mikaela, Aleah, Jahnaya, and three-week-old Beatriz. Leona and William Derden loaded up in three vehicles and slid their way here in the rough, wintry, end of January weather. Oh, what a wonderful thing to know that you're loved by your children. Being in the ministry, I've found out that many children do not care about their parents, they don't love them. I've served as the chaplain for the Pennington County Jail for a number of years. In that role, I heard some pretty horrible stories but my children love me!

My son (firstborn in the ministry), Elder Herman Hicks flew here, the very next day, along with Elder Ezzard Luke from Wichita, Kansas; Pastors Joseph and Cherri Lewis flew in from North Carolina where they lived at the time; Pastors Adrian and Susan Rodgers flew in from Jonesboro, Arkansas; Elder Jimmy Pierce drove here from the Tacoma, Washington area; Elder Matthew Mock of Wisconsin; Evangelist Sharon Colquitt of Warner Robbins, Georgia. These named here are ones who came through the ministry of Faith Temple Church in Rapid City except for the Rodgers. They were products of a prophetic word given to them when they visited our church, some years before, and the Lord had brought the prophetic words to fruition. These are my sons and daughters in the ministry. God is so good! God is so faithful! Also, our good friends, Bishop and Mrs. James Austin flew in from Chicago, Illinois. Our god daughter, Mae Hoffman flew in from Evanston, Illinois. Later on, Elder and Mrs. James Henderson drove here from Minot, North Dakota.

After coming out of the coma, I was surrounded by my close friends as they hugged on me and showered me with their love. My sons and their families were back in Minneapolis and traveling back and forth to see about me. When they weren't there, then, we visited by telephone, however, but my friends and church members were there for me and continued to visit, pray and whatever else it was that they could do. True friendship at it's very best.

Local pastors and members of other local churches were also among the throng of visitors who came, who cared and who conquered through prayer—I was told. With all of this, there were people of questionable motives who wanted to pray over me that were not allowed to do so. In fact, my wife later told me that she had to develop a strict Visitor's List and make sure the nurses monitored just who was allowed to enter my hospital room. There were very few who actually were allowed into the surgical intensive care ward to visit me, especially, while I was critically ill. They had to be on guard over all aspects and didn't want to take a chance on any new level of attack that the devil would launch against my chances of complete recovery. My wife worked with the hospital's Public Relations Department to not only monitor, but to control, just what the press would be allowed to print about my condition. She took my name off of the general information list so that no one could call in and obtain information about my condition. Whoever called or came by the hospital had to deal directly with my wife or her appointed representative who ever was on duty.

PRAYERS

Those mentioned above, along with our local church members and so many people from the Rapid City community who came to offer prayer, encouragement and support to my wife and family proved to be just what we needed! These all cried out to the Lord in my behalf. They held prayer vigils at the hospital in the Davies Family Waiting Room. On one day, in particular, Tuesday, January 31, I was going into surgery for the third time. My wife, the family, and friends all knew that my life was in grave danger since so much had happened already that should have left me dead, they thought that Satan would try especially hard to end my life this time. About eleven o'clock that morning, they began forming a hand clasped circle of prayer once every hour on the hour. They prayed that the Lord would spare my life—again. They prayed and rebuked the hand of death that seemingly was waiting to take me away. They fervently cried out to the Lord on my behalf. Praise the Lord! On that particular day, this strategically important day of prayer, a lady made a complaint to the Davies Waiting Room Attendant saying that we were frightening her with our praying and would she please ask them to move to another location? My wife responded in a very firm way and said, "No! We are not moving, we are going to stay right here and we are going to continue to pray for my husband's life. If they're uncomfortable then they can move to a different waiting room." Even in this, the devil was trying to interrupt the intercessory prayer and to scatter the people, but I believe that old saying, "Where there is unity, there is strength."

From that point on, they established a twenty-four-hour "watch" schedule with loved ones signing up to hold vigil in the Davies Room on a continuous schedule. People willingly and joyfully sacrificed many hours of their own precious time—both family and friends alike—to be there at the hospital and to keep me covered in prayer. The other reason was so that the medical team would always know there was someone (family or not) there that they could speak with about any of the numerous emergency situations that arose. If prayer was needed, then the person(s) on duty would make sure whatever the need was that it was handled. This person or persons was responsible for receiving the many telephone calls that came in; greeting the visitors and allowing them to leave a personal message to me in the Visitors Book created just for this occasion; speaking to the medical team if necessary; and miscellaneous other things. Those on night duty would bring their own blankets and pillows or just get them from the hospital. There was a section in the Davies Family Waiting Room that they took for their own—"The Kelly Section." Hot and cold meals were brought in for the family and friends. Flowers were delivered to their section (I could not receive them in my room due to the possibility of bacterial germs); Etc. I'm told that it was something to behold. On Saturday evening of the next week, our good friend and church member, Attorney Al Scovel, called and asked the Catholic church's bishop, Bishop Chaput to come and join them in prayer. As they were riding up in the elevator, he said, "Bishop Kelly is a saint!" And he repeated that three times. When he joined the prayer circle, he said, "God, heal Bishop Kelly. We need him here more than you need him there. Please heal and restore him to his full self!"

My wife, Evelyn! Thank God for her! She told me how the Lord guided her in all aspects of my care. The telephones were literally ringing off the hook everywhere—home, hospital, cell phones of any one that could give current information, etc. The Lord gave her the thought of placing a daily message on my cell phone with updates and prayer requests—daily! On the home number she left a message referring callers to the cell number, explaining that she was unable to answer or return all the calls that were coming in. Later, many people expressed their gratefulness at being able to know how intricately they could be involved through prayer. All over America, as well as internationally, the prayers went out and bombarded heaven. The Lord heard and answered. I am so grateful! **And Jesus lifted up his eyes, and said, Father, I thank thee that thou hast heard me. And I knew that thou hearest me always: but because of the people which stand by I said it, that they may believe that thou hast sent me."**—John 11:41-42

Chapter 3

DARKNESS

I had no idea of what had happened to me. All I remembered was the pain, it was so bad. I remember the ambulance ride to the Rapid City Regional's emergency room. I remember the pain, so much pain. After being placed in a curtained-off room and being examined, lots of questions from the nurses and doctors—they wheeled me down the hall for a CT scan and brought me back to the curtained-off room. The next time, I was rolled down that long hallway, it was for the surgery—the surgery of a lifetime! Just before being taken off for surgery, my wife asked me if I would speak to our eldest son, Thomas. Thomas was crying hysterically—such a big, giant of a man (six feet four and a half inches and more than three hundred pounds) but just a teddy bear. Well, I didn't understand what he was feeling because I didn't have a father. But I suppose just the threat of losing his father was too much for Thomas to bear—it really shook him up. My wife said, "Honey, Thomas is on the phone, can you talk to him?" I said, "Yes." When I answered the phone and heard the panic and the tears, I said, "What are you crying for? I'm the one in pain, not you!" Thomas replied, "I know Dad, but I'm just scared!" I answered, "I'll be all right, and I'll talk to you later." Needless to say, I had no idea just how much later it would be before I would be able to have another conversation with my family. Except for the miraculous grace and mercy of God, I might have never talked again, ever, in this life. I might never have seen again nor walked. I could have been a shell of a man unable to function in any capacity. Oh, the sweet grace and mercy of the Lord to *hear* and answer the prayers and tears of the people!

I remember being rolled down the hallway. I just remember being in a dark, dark place and I do not like darkness. As a matter of fact, I usually have a night light or a hallway light on when I sleep so that I can see something when I awaken. But I was in this dark place and I knew I wasn't alone. I was so comforted and I can just remember . . . Praise God! I remember hearing Evangelist Karen Clark-Sheard sing, '**IT'S NOT OVER TILL GOD SAYS IT'S OVER!**" That was a comfort to me because I didn't know where I was, I knew it . . . it was dark but I wasn't afraid because, it's not over until God says so—PRAISE GOD!

When I came fully awake, I was so tired of being in darkness and asked the Lord to bring me out of it. I was not afraid of the dark but I was weary of it. In that dark place, I began to quote the thirty-fourth Psalm. It's so wonderful that I had been taught to hide the Word of God in my heart. It was hidden in the crevices of my very being and even though I could not speak the words verbally, my spirit began to speak the words in my mind. **"This poor man cried, and the LORD heard him, and saved him out of all his troubles. The angel of the Lord encampeth round about them that fear him, and delivereth them. O taste and see that the LORD is good: blessed is the man that trusteth in him. O fear the LORD, ye his saints: for there is no want to them that fear him"**—Psalms 34:6-9. While I was crying out to the Lord from that dark place I said, "LORD, this deep, dark, horrible pit . . . please bring me out!" I heard the Bishop G. E. Patterson singing, "Look Where He Brought Me From." As confirmation of my cry, In the darkness, I could hear Loretta Oliver singing, "It Is Well" and "There Is No Failure in God"

IT'S NOT OVER UNTIL GOD SAYS IT'S OVER!

I remember one time the Lord came into my room. **HE** took me back to the Church of God in Christ Holy Convocation of 2005 in Memphis, Tennessee. My spirit was outside of my body. We were up in the ceiling inside the Cook Convention Center on the left side facing the audience looking down upon the people. **HE** told me to "look" and as I looked, the worship service was going on but people were eating, walking, talking on cell phones but most were not worshipping. I remember one lady in a real flashy outfit (I had noticed this person during the Convocation), well, I saw her again flashily dressed from head to toe as she went to her seat. I heard the Lord say "What have I to do with this?" Because people today are so casual about church, he said, "It is right to dress nice as you come before me but some of this is too much!" I remembered Mother Rivers asking, a few years ago, for the Women's Convention that the ladies would dress modestly and not so flashy so that they could really praise the Lord. *HE* said, "There are very few praisers and worshippers here." *HE* said, "Look around!" and it included the choir, it included the bishops, the supervisors, the General Board, and everybody all over the audience—it included all of the thousands who were present. *HE* said, "Bishop Patterson and Mother Rivers and the Saints come here and pray over the weekend before the Convocation and they ask me to come and every year I come!" And then *HE* said, "I leave because I'm looking for them to worship me and I'm not concerned about their clothes. I want to see the bishops, the supervisors, the General Board and the people praise **Me**. If they praise Me, I will come in their midst, I will bless them, and I will heal them" . . . Hallelujah! And, *HE* told me, "Tell them, tell them what I said." HE said, "Tell the bishops and the supervisors," "You ought to praise me because I am the one that raised you up. I raised you . . . I raised you!" *HE* said, "You ought to be praising me—you are blessed because of me!" *HE* said, "Tell Mother Rivers to lead the ladies in the dance—they'll dance and they will praise **Me**." The people are looking for examples and we can't just sit, we've got to praise God so the people will know that praise is comely!

One night of that particular Holy Convocation, Bishop Gerald Glenn was the speaker and a large delegation from his church had come to support him that evening. It just spoke of the love they have for their shepherd for so many of them to have taken the time to be with him. Anyway, he preached such a powerful message until all I could do was to sit and to cry—even after the message was over and the benediction had been pronounced. As the people were leaving the FedEx Forum by the thousands, I was constrained to remain in my seat sitting in the presence of the Lord. It was so great upon me and inside of me and I cried out to Him. "Oh God!" As they went past me, some of the bishops just patted me on the shoulder and one of them, briefly, sat down beside me and embraced me as if to comfort me. Still, all I could do was to cry because I felt that God was speaking to the Church of God in Christ through that powerfully prophetic message and it was the cry of my heart . . . "God, bring us back to holiness!"

The Holy Convocation was drawing to an end, now, and we were in Sunday's Official Day Service. Micah Stampley sang an anointed solo selection entitled "Holiness," and I tell you I stood in the presence of the Lord and I wept again. I was seated near the back of the bishops section and I was comfortable but I tell you, it just . . . that song brought me to my feet because, again, that is the cry of my heart. "Holiness is what I long for, Holiness is what I need!" After that selection was over, a little later in the service, Sister Karen Clark Sheard was called to minister the sermonic solo. As she approached the podium, she turned to address the late Presiding Bishop G. E. Patterson and said, "I believe that God told me to sing this song for you," and she began to sing, "IT'S NOT OVER UNTIL GOD SAYS IT'S OVER, IT IS NOT OVER TILL GOD SAYS IT'S OVER!" Again, I jumped to my feet—at this point, I didn't care what anyone thought of me. I grabbed that song for myself and the presence of the Lord just came and overwhelmed me again. Even though Sister Sheard had dedicated this selection to Bishop Patterson, I felt that the Lord was speaking directly to me through it. I had no idea what the future had in store for me but the Lord certainly did. I believe that He was already speaking to the devil in my behalf. God knew what was in store, what was to come upon me; and He alone knew the purpose of this tremendous testing. No matter what I was to go through, no one could count me out unless He did! It's not over until God says it's over!

Chapter 4

pleno jure

REVIVAL

In January of 2006, a week or so before my sudden, grave, illness, I was invited to preach revival services for the Fullness of Joy Ministries in Jonesboro, Arkansas. Pastors Adrian and Susan Rodgers, my children, are wonderful friends who the Lord brought into our lives many years ago. When we first met, they had come with a group of visitors to our church in Rapid City, SD. During their time in our worship services, the Lord had spoken to them prophetically about how He would use them in ministry in the years to come. Because the word of the Lord came to pass, in their leaders lives, their congregation members refer to me as their grandpa!

Anyway, in my humble opinion, I thought that this was one of the most powerful revival services I had ever done—to God be all the glory, honor and praise for His mighty acts! Salvation, healings and deliverances were the acts of the Lord witnessed during my five day stay beginning on Wednesday and ending on Sunday. During the final day, during the Sunday morning service I felt impressed by the Holy Spirit that an individual had a demonic stronghold that was operating in their life. I came against that demon and God gave us the power and the victory to cast it out! Not only that particular individual was delivered and set free to live a life of "holiness" unto the Lord but many others were ministered to through the anointing of the Holy Ghost—Praise God! After this service ended and lunch was finished, we went to an afternoon service at New Dimensions Church in Raleigh, Tennessee where Bishop Charles Rodgers (Adrian's father) is the pastor. I had been asked to speak for that service and again the Lord greatly honored me as he blessed the people again. It was a heavy schedule and who knew that, in exactly one week, I would be hanging between life and death. Who knew that a man who was ministering under the power and anointing of the Lord like this would be challenged in such a way in just a few short days?

We returned to Fullness of Joy for their evening service and my final sermon and ministry to this grandchildren congregation. Oh, the presence of the Lord was powerful. He swept in and people were crying out to Him, and, through the power of the Holy Spirit we ministered to almost everyone in the church, individually. Often, when I'm ministering at different churches, the pastors will freeze up if I happened to call out a demon; or if I address a sin issue that the Lord has brought to my attention. You know, when I call sin a sin, it doesn't mean that the church is bad; it just means that there are spiritual issues that must be dealt with and not tolerated. I've felt that some doors have been closed because of the call on my life and the type of ministry that I am exercised in. Sometimes, people have felt that they were being "picked" on personally and it has nothing to do with a person as much as what the Holy Ghost is doing.

I returned to the hotel tired but ever so satisfied that God had used me and that the people of the Lord were so greatly blessed. I did experience some heart palpitations and I had trouble getting my breath when I laid down to sleep so I sat up in the hotel room's recliner. I didn't think much about it just thought I might've been exhausted from the great amount of ministry that I had done over the past few days. I returned home to Rapid City early that week and kept up with my usual routine—time in the office and visitations to the Pennington County Jail inmates. On Friday night, the night before everything happened my wife and I had a nice romantic evening, stayed up late, watching movies and eating popcorn—it was good to be home.

WHAT HAPPENED?

When I awoke on Saturday morning, my wife was already up and getting ready for her busy day. I got up, took my medications, and started toward my wife's room to talk with her when I experienced unbelievable pain. Pain like I had never ever experienced racked my body (retired Physician, Dr.

Ray Strand, later told me that this is the absolute worse pain in the world). With my hand on my chest and a perplexed, startled look on my face, I said, "Honey, I'm in pain!" You've got to know my honey, my Evie, and if you do you'll know that she gets very excited very easily when anything out of the ordinary happens. She doesn't do that about herself but when the children were young, if anything happened to them, she would just come unglued. She asked, "What's the matter?" She exclaimed, "What's wrong?" I said, "I've got pain in my chest!" She told me to sit down and that she was going to call 911, and I protested, "I'll be all right." Then she demanded that, "You sit down, here!" pointing to the edge of the bed. I sat down and before calling 911, she had the wisdom to call Elder Troy Carr, the church's Assistant Pastor, explaining to him that I appeared to be having a heart attack. Well, that's the first thing most people would've thought of but, as we learned later, it was not a heart attack. Anyway, she asked Elder Carr to come right away to the house. She asked that, his wife, Evangelist Twana Carr would get over to the church as soon as possible to make sure everything was in place for the Women's Fellowship that was to happen that morning. She called 911. By this time, I had taken an aspirin and she helped me to walk down the hall and to sit down in my recliner chair.

By now, the intensity of the pain told me that I was in big trouble! I didn't know if I would live much longer but there was something I needed to say to my wife. It brings tears to my eyes even now but, even if it would be my last time to speak to her, I wanted her to know how much I loved her . . . that I loved her more than anything! I said, "Honey, I love you!" and then I spoke to the Lord and said, "Lord, You know I love You!" Then, the most unusual thing happened. From the pit of my belly the Holy Ghost . . . Praise God, began to speak in other tongues from deep down inside of me. The Holy Ghost was interceding for me in a language that we've never heard before or since it was amazing to hear such powerful words coming from the Holy Ghost Himself! Soon as He would let off speaking, I would repeat to my wife and to the Lord those words of love . . . "Honey, I love you!" and "Lord, You know I love You!" And then, the Holy Ghost would begin to speak again and this whole process continued over and over again. The 911 operator had remained on the line asking questions of my wife and giving her instructions and she could hear me speaking. Asking my wife to describe the level and source of the pain wracking my body, she then said, "What is he saying now?" My wife said, "He's speaking in unknown tongues. I'm not sure what he's saying." This went on and when I heard the ambulance sirens coming into our neighborhood. HE kept right on praying and interceding for me from the inside of my very being . . . Praise the Lord!

This is what happened to me—the Holy Ghost prayed the prayer that I needed to keep me alive. I never even thought of praying for myself during all that intense pain—never thought of it! However, prayer came out of my belly, my soul uttered in a language we've never heard before nor have we heard it since. I believe the Holy Ghost fought for my life and when Satan would have taken my life, the Lord said, "Not so!" I believe this, please don't think that I am big headed . . . I just feel like I had started to become a danger to him invading upon his territory in doing spiritual warfare for the Lord. I believe he wanted to move me out of his way—out of this world—and that a great battle was being waged over me! Well, that's what I believe! The presence of the Lord had been so powerful at that last revival and I had attacked a major stronghold of today. I have never really been sick before—no major sickness of any kind so this attack took me and my family by complete surprise! I see now. I understand that I was really supposed to be taken out! Supposed this attack had happened while I was alone in the hotel, what would have happened to me? Or even while traveling alone on the airplane or in the airport? God is so good to me! **"Likewise, the Spirit also helpeth out infirmities: for we know not what we should pray for as we ought: but the Spirit itself maketh intercession for us with groaning which cannot be uttered. And he that searcheth the hearts knoweth what is the mind of the Spirit, because he maketh intercession for the saints according to the will of God. And we know that all things work together for good to them that love God, to them who are the called according to his purpose"**—Rom. 8:26-28.

I've just got to say this here . . . this is why having the Baptism of the Holy Ghost is so important. Every believer needs the Holy Ghost abiding inside of them. The Holy Ghost empowers the believer. He is more than the experience of dancing, shouting and speaking in tongues—rather, HE brings POWER! HOLY GHOST POWER! He gives us authority. I know that I would not be alive today if HE had not stepped in on that Saturday morning. He held my life in His hands as he pleaded with the Lord for it. That is how I see that morning. **"Then he called his twelve disciples together, and gave them power and authority over all devils, and to cure diseases"**—Luke 9:1-2.

The paramedics were not able to get the stretcher all the way into my room, and so I told my wife, "I can walk over there, if it's okay." Even though the pain was so bad and I was groaning and rocking because of it, I was still able to get up, walk over to the stretcher, sit down, and then lie down on it. Look at God! Elder Carr arrived just at this time as they were bringing me out of the house on the stretcher. He asked if he could ride along with me in the ambulance and they said he could. My wife said, "Honey, I'll be right on!" and so I said, "Okay." My son Troy, that's what I call him, held my hand and tried to comfort me. The Holy Ghost . . . **HE** kept right on praying and I thought again, "Hmmm, the Psych Hospital is closer to my house than the Regional Hospital. Hope they don't take me to the wrong one (smile)." I said to the Lord, "You've got to stop this because they'll think I'm crazy and take me to the mental hospital" (Smile). But **HE** just kept right on . . . bless His wonderful Name! **"Likewise the Spirit also helpeth our infirmities: for we know not what we should pray for as we ought: but the Spirit itself maketh intercession for us with groaning which cannot be uttered"**—Rom. 8:26.

I wondered why it was taking so long for the ambulance to get to the hospital. They are usually going zoom-zoom fast whenever you see them around town but this one seemed to be very slow. I was lying there looking out the window at the trees, etc., and I heard them discussing that they were waiting for a doctor that was supposed to catch up with the ambulance. Anyway, I guess he had gone past our subdivision on up West Highway 44, but he never did find us before we finally arrived at Emergency.

LIFE

After the CT Scan was completed it was diagnosed that I was in the midst of having an aneurysm of the thoracic aorta. They didn't know, at that point, just how extensive the surgery would need to be but Dr. Gordon explained that they would follow the "tear" and repair only as much as was needed. He said that he was grateful that the flap had not blown and they were going to do everything that they could to save my life but that this was a very grave situation. He further told my wife that because of the way the pain initially began, that I really could have had a massive brain stroke and died immediately. If it had branched up into the carotid arteries into my head, I would have been out of here! OH! BUT GOD! **It's not over until God says that it is over!**

DEATH

The cardiac surgeon, who was the attending physician in the operating room, Dr. Robert Gordon, later told my wife that I had died five times on the operating table and they had to bring me back over and over again. They fought for my life! In the process of keeping me alive, having frozen my body for the surgery, they had to place heat around me to get my blood warmed up and moving again. Inadvertently, I sustained severe burns to the front of both legs (it was later learned they were fourth degree burns) as the surgical and medical team continued to fight to restore and retain my life. The flap that connects the aorta to the heart did not blow—THANK GOD! However, the aneurysm (tear in the inner lining) started just off from the flap and continued to rip way down to above my renal organs. At the conclusion of the ten hour surgery, they had done a number of tremendous things to my body and the main thing was replacing eighteen inches of my aorta with man-made materials. The medical records of this surgery are included in this book and you will be, simply, amazed at the expertise of what that surgical team was able to do. I was in the first surgery from 12:30 PM until 10:30 PM on Saturday, January 28. Even though I came through the surgery, Dr. Gordon explained that only 10 percent of people make it through this type of surgery and then he would say, "He's in the 10 percent, but he's not out of the woods yet." Further, of the 10 percent who make it through the surgery, some may still die of one kind of complications or another. Dr. Gordon's greatest disclaimer that he would tell my family over and over again was that "It is up to the Man upstairs!" As he would say it, he would point up toward the ceiling. They knew that he meant God.

The next time that life and death was so crucial was during the second surgery early that Sunday morning. You know that this is all just hearsay but this is what Sister Leonne Seevers told me about the doctors summoning our sons and telling them, "You'd better come now if you want to see him alive. We've got to take him into surgery again because we've discovered a blood seepage but we don't know where it's coming from. We have to locate it and stop it. We don't know if he'll make it or not, it's up to the

Man upstairs." I was taken back into surgery at around 2:00 AM until about 8:00 AM that morning—they were able to find and stop the seepage. Still, they explained to my family that, "He's not out of the woods yet!" and "It's up to the Man upstairs, now!"

The next time that life and death was so crucial was during the third surgery on the following Tuesday afternoon. On Saturday night when the first surgery was over, Dr. Gordon told my wife that they were not able to stitch my chest closed due to the large amount of fluids that were in my body. He said, "Every time we started to sew him up, he would start to die again . . . so we've left him open for now. We'll have to give him twenty-four-hour dialysis to pull off the massive amount of fluids that are in his body before we can stitch him up. This will probably take a few days, probably not before Tuesday but we'll let you know." My wife said that my chest was wrapped in a cellophane type of material and that she could see my heart pumping through the opening.

Immediately, sometime that Sunday, they began the first twenty-four-hour dialysis—the first of several dialysis treatments and were able to reduce the fluid level in my body but there would need to be more. I received several more dialysis treatments over the next two days to get me ready for the surgery to close the sternum and the first debridement of the burns on my legs. The medical records say that the surgery went fine but that I suddenly went into cardiac arrest after I was back in my room. There was no time to get the families permission to save my life—they just did it, shocking and working over my body for a few hours.

I remember feeling like I had no pride left while being in intensive care. I have always enjoyed my privacy but I learned that in the hospital there is no such thing as privacy. It's more like, turn over, bend over, wetting the bed, having no control over our bodily functions. Some of the staff don't expect you to do better and you can't was all something new to me. Being dependent on someone else like a baby was new to me. I didn't like it! Young eighteen or nineteen year old girls would come into my room to bathe me. Hold on to the rail Bishop Kelly, turn to the right side, now to the left, my privacy was gone! Later, it was Franceen, Elder Carr who did the same thing. Elder Carr started teasing me saying he knew everything. There was no time to be embarrassed, because it all had to be done.

When they started giving me food to eat, I did not want it. Food was repugnant to me. I did not want it so my wife started bringing me juice drinks from home and then she would stay with me all night, get up early in the morning go home get ready for the day and also cook my breakfast and lunch and bring it back to me. I got where I knew when she was walking down the hallway. I would hear her walking and say here comes my wife. She had become my reason for living! I would eat a few bites and stop so who ever was taking care of me would threaten to tell her if I did not eat. That was the way they got food into me.

Chapter 5

Sans peur et sans reproche

WHAT DOES IT MATTER?

Oh, I cannot tell you the order of the events of His visitations to me but what an awesome experience I've had with the Lord! **"And I saw the dead, small and great, stand before God; and the books were opened: and another book was opened, which is the book of life: and the dead were judged out of those things which were written in the books, according to their works."**—Rev. 20:12

Let me tell you that story. I was taken in one of my visitations with Jesus up to a classroom. It looked like one of the old fashioned ones that I saw or knew in the South. Jesus had a **Book of Life** and written in that Book was all the hidden hurts of my life. Hurts from church, from home, misunderstandings, things that I'd done and that I had regretted—just on and on and on—these things were listed on the board. He wanted to rehearse it and he told me to read it and I read it and **HE** said, "What do you think of this?" and I said, "Lord, it doesn't matter cause I'm with You!" Then I realized that all the deeds that we think that we have gotten over, those things that are still alive in us. It was on the board. He went to number two, and **HE** said, "Well, does this matter?" and I said, "Lord, it doesn't matter!" and He went all down the list on that board to the very end. My disappointments, how people have walked away from us, from the ministry; how people made promises to support us; how people relayed the evil that somebody had said about us and the ministry; and the abuse that I suffered as a child. Oh . . . He took everything away and I came back here free and trying to tell people, in my little squeaky voice, telling them, "What does it matter?"

I AM FREE!

Being in the classroom with the Lord made such a big difference and left a lasting impact upon my life. He paid special attention to, dealt with and banished the effect of the memories that had followed me most of my life. Then, I understood that if I had memories that plagued me then so did others and He was sending me back to preach and minister freedom to others as He had done to me. Saints, when we finally get the opportunity to be with the Lord, all of life's stuff that we have built an altar to will mean nothing to us. Many times, because the pains of life have been so great and so horrific, we tend to build an altar and we begin to worship those hurts as if it they were an idols of worship. To be more specific, most of us hold onto the sin of "un-forgiveness" and we hold it so close to our hearts until it's literally impossible to give it up. Sometimes, we feel that because we've been victimized that we have a right to be angry and to not forgive. What we don't realize is that the person who is hurt the most is ourselves. Additionally, because we are Christians and we have been taught that it is right to forgive, many of us will go through the motions and will say that we have forgiven those who offended us. However, many times it is just words and not the action of forgiveness. When we hold onto un-forgiveness, when *we do not forgive*, then we bind those sins done to us into ourselves in our actions or personality.

When I returned to my hospital room, I knew what being set free really meant. Yes, those old feelings and memories try to come back to me but I continue to remind myself that I have been set free and I don't want to let un-forgiveness rule my life! When it is time for us to be with the Lord in heaven—nothing else should matter except being with Him! He is the GREAT I AM!

NOT HALLUCINATIONS!

I know twice I was out of here when they put me on the dialysis machine. I know that even in the hospital room when I was lying there in darkness, God was there and he spoke to me. I can tell you one thing for sure and that is that Satan has tried his best to steal my testimony. I can tell you that I've had to fight him because he said that I imagined it! Whatever! I know what I saw and experienced . . . I'm like that man in Acts 4:20 . . . Praise God! Peter and John said, "For we cannot but speak the things which we have seen and heard . . ." I've had people tell me that I was hallucinating but I beg to differ with that! I didn't hallucinate—I saw and heard these things for myself and, oh, did I experience the presence of the Lord!

Now, I remember another time and I now know that it was one of the times that I was receiving a dialysis treatment. I was out of my body, again and on a ship down in the lounge area. People were so happy and so excited and I was just smiling. I was sitting at a booth by myself. See, when you die, you don't take anyone with you—you die by yourself. I was sitting at that lounge table by myself and somehow I knew that I was going to sing. I had knowledge, but I don't know how I knew. But my voice was gone! I said, "Lord, I'm on this program and—I can't. I can't sing! You've got to touch my voice—touch my voice!" Well, the next thing I knew, I was up in the air, and I was floating—oh, such a wonderful feeling. Just wonderful! I was spinning and all of a sudden I was at my aunt's house and, seemingly, my mother's house combined—my family members were there. I was trying to tell them something that the Lord was saying to them but they could not hear me.

I have found the importance of writing because Satan has attacked my mind and tried to take my testimony over and over again. He wants me to think that what I've experienced was imagined and not real. So I am writing and I will remember this forever! I remember what God has done for me and I thank Him for it. I thank him for the people that God has used—Praise God—to strengthen me. Also, I thank God for the ones who caused me problems during this time, even those relayed in my ears. I'll never forget that that one word that a brother in the Lord said to me. He visited our church during a Sunday evening service and I was telling about what the Lord had done for me. After the service was over, he came over to speak with me and he said, "You know I was very ill, also, over the past few months. I understand what happened to you because I hallucinated too." Right there I knew that Satan was using this brother to shut up my testimony but I will not be shut up. I will always tell of the goodness of Jesus and what He has done for me—always! If it were a hallucination then people wouldn't be blessed by the testimony as I share it. I have seen people crying and weeping and grabbing onto what God has said to me. When they do, the Lord delivers them from the power and bondage of Satan. I know it's not a hallucination, hallelujah it's JESUS!

My recovery was so long and so weary. I would get so tired and just pray. I prayed and ask God to give me my strength back for I was as small as I had been forty-one years ago when my wife and I got married. I was down to about a fourteen-and-a-half-inch neck size—so small. God was so faithful, and over time, I have regained my health and my strength—and my size (smile).

I now know that the Lord was teaching me empathy for those who have suffered and been sick. So often when we pray for the sick, we command them to be healed and often times do not understand how this person feels. Especially when they ask for prayer again and again and you're thinking that they should just believe God and get on with it!

RESTORATION

For the first couple of weeks, I was kept under heavy sedation, on a ventilator for life support and hanging somewhere between life and death, critically ill. I didn't know where I was but I remember hearing the bells ringing, over and over again. Those bells had something to do with the life support Ventilator unit but it seemed they would never stop ringing. I was in that dark place for a long time, it seemed, and I felt so alone at one point. I remember being out of my body one time during the early hospital stay and being in this beautiful place. I thought I was in some part of Nebraska near the Sand Dunes. I remember it being so beautiful, quiet and peaceful. I remember wondering why my family had not come to get me. I did not know that the doctors were fighting for my life. I never imagined that I would be in the hospital for more than a few hours. I had expected them to find nothing wrong with me, after all, had not the Holy Ghost been with me up until we arrived at the hospital? I just knew that everything was going to be all right.

When I began to become awake and more aware of things and people around me, I began to experience something unusual. I believe because I was so close to the other world that I could still see things that you don't usually see with the normal eye. When someone would come into my room, I would see a color behind them. I was now able to try to write and I sloppily wrote a note to my wife that said, "I see the meanest of people in colors." I would try to tell her about the mean spirits some people have because I could see them. Sometimes the Holy Spirit would tell me not to touch them or allow them to touch me. At other times, with my weak and raspy voice, I would warn a person about getting right with the Lord. I still see things and recognize the spirit working in people—I just don't say anything many times.

Later, I was able to pray with some to receive the Lord into their lives—yes! While still striving to recover I was still trying to do my work for the Lord. He is so good! One of the nurses asked me to tell him about the Baptism of the Holy Spirit. He said that he believed the Lord had me there for him. During my time in the medical intensive care unit (I had graduated up from the surgical intensive care unit), and when visitors would come to see me the Lord would use me to minister to them.

Upon coming completely awake and after all the sedations were discontinued, I was having trouble seeing. My vision was unclear and my eyeglasses seemed useless. Like they were someone else's prescription so I'd just take them off immediately after putting them on—it was no use since I couldn't see out of them! By now, I had graduated and been moved into the pulmonary unit out of the medical intensive care unit. An eye specialist was summoned to examine my eyes and he discovered that I had suffered two strokes in the left eye and three strokes in my right eye. This had happened during the first surgery when I was frozen and blood supply was not able to reach my eyes. So, it looked like a pretty sad prognosis for me and it was very upsetting. This took place on a Friday, a few days before I would be released to Rehab.

I prayed and believed the Lord would take care of this problem for me and heal these eyes. After all, I had seen him heal other people's eyes before, so, naturally I expected the same for myself. Early the next morning, another Saturday morning—things happen on Saturday mornings, y'all! So early the next morning, when I awakened and tried to see, I couldn't. I was so upset and told the Lord that I wasn't talking to Him anymore. Later, I heard Him call my name and say, "Lorenzo, put the glasses on." Well, these were the same glasses that the doctor had examined me with just the night before when I could not see through them well. However, I obeyed. I put them on and even though the doctor had given me no hope for improvement I could now see through them. PRAISE THE LORD! In fact, over time my eyes improved so much until my vision is now stronger than it was before I became ill. Like I said, PRAISE THE LORD!

CURSING

I was able to write and tell my wife some of the things that I wanted to say. I realized that I had lost my ability to remember how to spell, some simple words and I had trouble spelling them. But even though I would misspell them, they would still decipher what I was trying to say. I had felt so guilty about the cursing, that I mentioned earlier, and had apologized to the Lord until I wrote my wife a note about it—this was before I could speak again. The note said, "I think I have learned how to curse." And I told her about being in this dark place and cursing, and I was telling Jesus, "Oh, I'm sorry, I usually don't talk this way, and I don't know what happened I guess I've learned how to curse." I was pretty concerned about that and knew that it wasn't like me to use swear words. One day, my wife and Franceen met with the doctor and his surgical team in order to have them explain how it was that I was burned during the first surgery. As they were discussing the dire emergency they were functioning under and explaining those details, they said that someone forgot to watch the heater that was over my legs. There was so much going on and, Dr. Gordon said, "He died five times on the table and we had to place him on cardiopulmonary bypass a couple of times. We were all concentrating on his chest problems. Because he was frozen, there was no circulation in the legs. The heat wasn't on him very long but due to a lack of circulation and nothing to move the blood, the burns happened very quickly."

My wife got a bright idea because she, too, could not imagine that I would actually be cursing. She asked, "Say. When you're in those surgical settings and things are so tense do the doctors sometimes curse when they're in the operating room?" They looked pretty guiltily from one to the other and the head nurse took on a sheepish grin and answered, "Yes, we do!" She replied, "Well, some of those patients can hear you. My husband thought he was cursing and he will be so relieved to know that it wasn't him, after all!" They all got a laugh off of that. Even though I was embarrassed about the cursing I still wanted to be truthful about it. When she told me I was very relieved, and said, "Whew, it wasn't me after all!" PRAISE THE LORD!

Chapter 6

mirabilia

STAGES

On January 28, 2006, I had an aneurysm of the thoracic aorta. From what I've learned about aneurysms—in the worst case, an aneurysm can burst, or rupture. This causes severe pain and bleeding. It often leads to death within minutes. An aortic aneurysm can also lead to other problems—blood flow often slows in the bulging section of an aortic aneurysm, causing clots to form. If a blood clot breaks off from an aortic aneurysm in the chest area, it can travel to the brain and cause a stroke. It is not an option to wait until an aneurysm has ruptured before surgery is done. Most people who have a ruptured aortic aneurysm die. Surgery for an already ruptured aneurysm may be tried but it is not usually successful due to excessive blood loss.

Okay, here are the stages of my hospitalization: I was in surgical intensive care for almost three weeks—January 28 through February 25; I was in medical intensive care and pulmonary care for about a week—February 25 through March 3; and I was in the rehabilitation hospital from March 3 through March 15. I returned to the Rapid City Regional Hospital for the final skin graft surgery on March 31 through April 8. Again, I was admitted to the hospital from May 16 through 18 due to an *E. coli* infection in the left knee.

The medical team had to battle from many so many different fronts—almost every day for a while, there was some kind of surgical procedure needed to be performed on me. Additionally, I contracted the hospital borne MRSA and the MRSE bacterial infections while in surgical and medical intensive care units. If you have ever heard the news about those infections you'll realize, along with me, that here was another opportunity for death to overtake me. According to an article in the Rapid City Journal on Sunday, July 28, 2008, here are some statistics about those infections:

> "In 2005, the most recent data available, more than 94,000 Americans developed a serious MRSA infection. About 18,650 people died during a hospital stay of causes related to those infections. People sixty-five years old or older were most at risk."

MRSA is an antibiotic-resistant bacteria "superbug" known as methicillin-resistant staphylo-coccus aureus. Invasive MRSA kills. That means the bacteria has entered the blood, brain, spinal fluid or other sterile place. Being over-treated for viral infections can help cause a person to get MRSA. Several months before my sickness, I had been being treated with several differ-rent antibiotics for flu like symptoms that would not come under control. One of the antibiotics was Levaquin and according to its side effects, that medication could have contributed to my having the aneurysm but no one actually discussed this with me until after everything had happened. Anyway, by God's grace and mercy the medical team was able to keep me alive even though I contracted this deadly bacterial infection.

I had multiple blood transfusions during the process of the surgeries. Within the first few days of my hospitalization, my wife requested the Infections Control physician to test me to find out whether or not I had contracted the Legionnaires disease and, perhaps, that was why I'd had the aneurysm. You see, between June and October of 2005, many people in our community had become sick from air spores breathed in from a beautiful water-fountain located in the lobby of a local restaurant. Our mayor, at that time, was one of those people who not only were deathly ill but he had to have open heart surgery from complications of the disease. The reason she was concerned was because of the fact that we had eaten in that same restaurant in August and I had come down with those flu-like symptoms in September and my doctor tried one antibiotic after another to conquer this condition. Because my blood had already been changed out, multiple times, during the surgeries, they were unable to conclude whether or not Legionnaires Disease might have caused this aneurysm of the thoracic aorta.

LEARNING

While I was in the medical intensive care and the pulmonary care units one of the therapists decided to encourage me to begin to try to walk. I was afraid of falling but she encouraged me by saying to me, "You CAN do it!" as I leaned on the walker and as she held onto the support clamped around my waist. After the initial weak starts and stops, I was able to go around the Nurses Station one time, with her help and her sweet encouragement. She must have known that I was a man of "faith!" and, I'm sure this was the Lord using her to pull me up to a new level of recovery and restoration. After the second time around was completed, she said to me, "Bishop Kelly, would you like to try it one more time?" By that time, I had the courage and the strength to do so and I said, "Yes!" and we went around the third time.

One morning right after I started learning how to walk again, an attendant came to get me from the hospital room. He and the nurse helped me into the wheelchair and I was taken to X-Ray. When I got there, I was told to stand in front of the screen. Neither the attendant nor the X-Ray Technician reached out to help me to stand so I tried it on my own and began to fall. What the attendant did not realize was that the other person who had followed me down to the X-Ray Lab was with me. This was during the time that my wife assigned members of our church to stay overnight to watch over my care. Since this was early the next morning, Sister Leonne Seevers was still there. She's white so none of the hospital staff even questioned who she was. She doesn't look like me, skin-color wise, but she calls me Dad! So, she asked the attendant, "What's wrong? Are you afraid to touch my dad?" He quickly apologized, he had thought that I was alone and so it didn't really matter if he wasn't doing his job properly or not. When he realized that I was not alone, his attitude and care of me was different immediately. I would have been hurt very badly if I had fallen because of their neglect. Again, God is awesome and his grace and mercy is great!

CHOKING AND GASPING

The ventilator and breathing tube, unknowingly, became my best friends for quite a while. It was later learned that one of my vocal cords was damaged because the breathing tube was left in longer than was desirable. It was necessary that it be left in place because there were other medical situations that were being dealt with. When they were finally able to remove the breathing tube they performed a tracheotomy and then it was necessary to perform regular suctioning out of the clots and phlegm/sputum that formed constantly, it seemed. I was still not really conscious of everything that was happening but life preservation kicked in and I would grab the suctioning tool and try to clear out the phlegm and clots. Many times, there was so much until it would string out in long, clotty bunches—often I would have to ring for the nurse to come in and help me get my breathing passages clear. This condition continued from the time I was in medical-surgical intensive care until I had been moved into the pulmonary ward. One night, in particular, my wife was sitting with me and the male nurse assigned to my ward was in and out. He would stop into my room briefly to explain that he would be back as soon as possible. He said he was very busy working this ward and one on another floor. At one point, I began to choke and gag on the phlegm it was so much until I just couldn't get it all out. Evelyn rang the buzzer for the nurse and began to try to help get it all out as she, intermittingly, rang the buzzer again and again. Thank God she was there because I don't think I could have succeeded getting myself clear without her help. After about thirty minutes, the nurse showed up again Evelyn told him what had happened, however, he didn't seem particularly alarmed about it. You know, everything seemed like a crisis and like a potential life hazard. That was one of the continued alarming episodes that kept me just this side of panic.

REHABILITATION

When I was sent to Rehab, a nurse's assistant came to get me. Her name was Linda. I soon realized that the Lord had set this in order as well. She was really a sister in the Lord, a real believer. She got me settled in my room and for the next two weeks when she was on duty, which was almost every day, she would try to see about me. Even if she wasn't assigned to my section she would still come in to pray with me and check on me. The first few days, when the enemy would attack me, she would pray over me. She's from West Virginia with a strong accent and she was not taking any stuff from Satan as she walked into my room in Holy Ghost authority and began to pray. "Get out of here, Devil! You have no right to touch the Lord's anointed!" Whenever I felt like I couldn't she would remind me that I could. Some days, she would preach a fair sermon while she washed me up and dressed me.

After being moved to rehab, I began to suffer dizzy spells and would break out in a heavy sweat and have to lie down in the bed. I would fall asleep and later awake with the bed clothes soaked. Yet the therapist thought I was faking. Why would I be faking when I wanted to finish therapy and get out of that place and go home? I just wanted to go home! Evelyn to the rescue! She began to go through all my medication and questioned the staff about what they were giving me. She had discovered they were giving me too much of one thing or another.

One day, near the beginning of my stay in Rehab, I needed help to get out of bed to go to the bathroom. I rang the buzzer and waited and waited and waited! When no help came, I tried to get to the bathroom on my own but didn't have enough strength to get out of the bed. As I was lying halfway in and halfway out of the bed, I urinated on myself. I will never forget the RN slowly coming into the room, leaning against the wall, standing there watching me as I struggled to keep from falling off of the bed onto the floor. She asked if she could help me—it was obvious that I needed help but with the attitude that I sensed on her, I didn't want her help. I asked her to send Linda in to help me. I later placed a formal complaint against that nurse. Sister Linda took such loving care of me and kept me in prayer.

There were other nurses both in the hospital as well as in rehab who were Christians—both male and female. They readily prayed for me and encouraged me with their Christian witness. My wife told me of one nurse "Cathy" in those early intensive care days that held me, prayed for me and sang to me during such a touch and go time while I was critically on life support.

It was just a few days after transferring into the Rehabilitation Hospital and I'd had a particularly hard and painful morning. Evelyn had met with the Rehab Social Worker to discuss my ongoing care and by the time she left that office, walked down the hall, and came into my room she found me in a very frustrated way! I don't remember when this started but I remember receiving morphine shots before the debriding treatments and waiting for the doctor to come to debride the burn areas. It seemed that the doctor would always come after the medicine had worn off and would proceed with his treatment anyway. The pain would be so bad but the doctor would just chew his gum and act as if I was not in pain. Day after day this continued to happen and I would cry and ask the Lord why I had to go through this. One day I just cried out to Him, heal me or kill me and I meant it! She said that I looked up at her and I shouted out these words . . . "I TOLD THE LORD TO KILL ME OR HEAL ME!" There was something so determined while at the same time so desperate in this declaration. There was no fear in it, just decision. I knew that God could do and would do whatsoever was His will and I was willing to die or to be healed. No in betweens!

In Rehab I had to learn how to walk again as well as how to take care of myself. Sister Linda Ault, Sister Franceen Robinson and other volunteers were my day sitters while I was in intensive care and in rehab. Elder Troy Carr, Attorney Al Scovel, Elder Lawrence Cliette, my wife, Evelyn and others usually covered the night shifts. They tried to always have someone present to sit with me so that I could be taken care of in an excellent way. One day, another patient's parents approached Sister Ault and asked her if, "Bishop Kelly would come down to our son's room and pray for him." Their fourteen year old son had been in a skateboarding accident and was a paraplegic unable to do almost nothing for himself. Even though I still needed help walking and getting around, I was willing to go and minister to this young teenager. Even though I still had my own questions about my own situation I still believed that the Lord would make a way somehow! After struggling my way down the hall, I went into that room and prayed for him and his parents—I've

Photography by Franceen Robinson

This "Divine Seal" of God appears on ↑ Bishop Kelly's left shoulder as he preaches his first message to his congregation. This "Seal" is a mysterious phenomenon that has shown up in several photos. It signifies "The Truth of the Lord!".

never heard from them since then but I believe that God honored us and provided some means of encouragement to that family.

After my discharge from Rehab, I was planning to be in church the next Sunday but the Lord allowed a big snow storm to come through and so we stayed in. Oh, but the next Sunday, I went to church. I had to be pushed in a wheelchair and helped to walk the few steps into the pulpit. The chairs were arranged so that I could preach while sitting and facing the congregation. I preached and encouraged the saints on that day. We had a great reason to rejoice in the Lord because He had spared my life and brought me back into the sanctuary again.

At home, I required around the clock nursing care and, again, Sister Linda Ault along with Sister Franceen Robinson assisted my wife, Evelyn, in making sure everything was handled for me. There seemed to be hundreds of medications that I had to take on certain schedules—my wife managed that. My bloody legs, hips and thighs were raw and those dressings had to be changed two to three times a day. Home Health Nurses came in to do that and to attend to my bathing, along with Sister Franceen. Because of the open wounds from the skin graft donor sites and from the burn sites, it was weeks before I could actually get in the tub for a shower or a bath. As well they were to help with any medical or prescription situation. The doctors wanted me off of my feet as much as possible because of the swelling and the healing issues. However, on one Sunday in particular, I was standing in the pulpit *P R E A C H I N G !* when a Rapid City Journal photographer came in and snapped a picture of me giving out the Word of the Lord to the congregation. Later that week, I ended up in an emergency situation having contracted an bacterial infection in my left knee. My Plastic Surgeon said, "Oh, yes, I saw that picture of you on the front page of the paper! Hmm . . . you were standing weren't you?" I dropped my head and answered, "Yes, I was."

After receiving the last skin grafts, I had received home treatments until the skin was healed enough for me to wear stockings which were made to fit me up to the waist and, later, to fit over the legs and thighs. They had to be tight enough to make the swelling go down and stay down in the skin only and the abrasions were sometimes up to a half an inch thick—a little like leather. So, the support hose had to do a double job—give my legs support and try to eliminate the thickness. The thickness did not go away so my attorney found a doctor who gave me treatments and injections to eliminate the thickness. These were steroid shots, and the first few treatments were performed at the Same Day Surgery Center. It seemed like I was never going to get away from the hospital as this went on for several months. Later on, the treatments were done at the doctor's office. Some of those shots were so painful and it seemed as though I would never get done with pain as being a part of my life.

Chapter 7

omnia vincit amor

DEPRESSION

As a young man I had suffered from depression. Teen life was not easy and I had no one to talk to about my feelings. Yet, the depression that I felt during recovery and sometimes since cannot compare to those times. While in the hospital, the doctors offered me medication for depression but I did not understand why. I felt like I was all right and me and the Lord could handle anything. Once I had received the final skin graft surgery to my legs and all the infections had been dealt with, I felt like I was on the mend. Never realizing that now my spirit had to deal with what had happened to me and in some ways, this was as terrifying to me. All of a sudden I was asking me **WHAT HAPPENED TO ME? WHERE HAD ALMOST TWO MONTHS GONE? WHY, WHAT HAD I DONE TO HAVE TO GO THROUGH SO MUCH SUFFERING?**

Depression came upon me in a big way! I would just break and cry at a moment's notice. Once I went to my doctor's office and the nurse wanted to take some blood and when I saw the needle, I just broke and cried. My poor veins had been stuck so many times until they had gone into hiding. A psychologist friend sent word to me that if I needed him to let him know. Never in my wildest imaginations would I ever have thought I would be seeking out a psychologist! Yet, I was crying so much and, mentally, feeling so bad until I went to see him.

Yes, I was going to church and preaching on Sundays, praying for the sick and the Lord was moving in a marvelous way. But there I was fighting with depression. I felt like I was becoming King David's brother. I found out later that depression is normal for people who have gone through traumatic illnesses or situations. Yes, we are men and women of God and, yes, we love the Lord, BUT, we are still human beings. Remember the Prophet Elijah after winning a great battle against the prophets of Baal. When he received a threatening letter from Jezebel, he runs for his life and goes into depression. I could definitely relate to King David and the Prophet Elijah. However, after a number of visits and taking the prescribed medications, obeying the doctor, the depression broke. I was able to get off of the medication but even to this day, I still sometimes have to fight it.

THE IMPORTANCE OF SONGS

Now, I want to talk about the song that Sister Karen Clark Sheard sings, "It's Not Over Till God Says It Is Over!" I heard that song in that dark place. Even before the dark place, remember this was one of the songs that ministered to me so greatly just about three months before all this happened. I never realized that there are two vocal cords in our throats but I became aware of that after learning that one of my vocal cords had been damaged because of the tubing that was in my throat for an extended period of time. In fact, after examination of my vocal cords I was told that it would take at least a year to regain my voice. That, in time the good vocal cord would take over for the bad one but until that time I would only be able to speak in a raspy, small voice. You know, Satan's so crazy to think I going to be preaching in a weak, raspy voice for a year or more! Hmmph!

After being out of the hospital, at home recovering and now able to speak a little more clearly, I made a telephone call to Superintendent Drew Sheard, her husband, apologized for disturbing him and told him about my experience and about hearing Karen singing that song while I was in that dark place. I asked him, "Would you please find your wife, if she's in town, and tell her what a blessing that song was while I was in that dark place. Ask her if she would please give me a call. I also asked him to please call Evangelist Dorinda Clark Cole, as well. Maybe it was five or ten minutes or so, it wasn't very long until Karen Clark Sheard was on my phone. I told her what a blessing that song was. I believe we ought to tell people now how we feel and how they've blessed us instead of waiting to say it at a funeral or when saying it just for attention. Tell them so they would be encouraged and they would know the anointing that was on the song. So, when I was finished sharing with her she thanked me and said, "Now, before I get off the phone can I pray for you?" I almost fainted! She said, "I want to pray for you." As she prayed, **she asked the Lord to do for me what he had done for her.** A few years earlier, the doctors had given her a two percent chance to live when she was very ill. I don't know what her exact experience was because I don't know her that well. So, I didn't know what her experience was but I knew that I didn't have my full voice. I had been praying, asking Him, "God, give me my voice back, please, Lord! Let me dance again! Heal these legs!" Well, while I was talking with her my cell phone beeped and it was her sister, Dorinda Clark Cole. I finished talking to her and went to my wife's office and said, "Well, she not only listened to me, she prayed for me." Can you imagine a professional gospel singer who prays under the anointing of the Holy Ghost? She really knows the Lord!

FEAR

During my stay at the hospital, I was introduced to an emotion that I had never had a real problem with before. FEAR! I can remember not wanting to go to sleep because I had been away from life for so long. I wondered if I fell asleep, would I wake up. At the same time, sleep was my friend because when I was asleep I didn't have to deal with the pain. Also, when I was sent home, Fear followed me there. It is strange, because I was afraid to die because that had already happened to me. On one hand, I felt that death was always there during those months between May and October. I felt so close to death that all I had to do was agree with death and I would be gone. There was a part of me that wanted to go back to be with the Lord. At the same time, I didn't want to leave Evelyn and my family. I had discovered a depth of love in her that I never expected to ever want or experience. I found myself not wanting to ever be without her always wanting her near. Feeling safe and secure when she was around, and waking up in the middle of the night just to look at her. I had thought, before this, that I loved her but I can't even describe how I feel about her today. This woman of God called me back from death. I was glad to be going back to the Lord and I heard her voice as she called me back to her. I found myself being afraid I would leave her again. Afraid of Death, No! Afraid to leave Evelyn, Yes!

"I will bless the LORD at all times: his praise shall continually be in my mouth. I sought the LORD, and he heard me, and delivered me from all my fears"–Psalms 34:2, 4.

RELATIONSHIP

I am so thankful and grateful that the Lord has mended my relationship with my brother. While I was with the Lord, I told him that my brother really didn't know me because of some things that had happened between us and we were not getting along. The Lord said to me, "You don't know him either." So when I got home from the hospital, he was one of the persons I wanted to see. My sister Barbara insisted that the two of them would join my sister Neva and my own family at Easter in my home. After Easter service, we sat together and talked. All I wanted both my sisters and my brother to know was that I love them. My family means the world to me. I had learned a very important about life! Say what you need to say to them, be quick to forgive, love, love, love and enjoy each day, one day at a time. One sure lesson I learned was that we have no time to waste! I have not been able to reconcile in my mind how I went to bed feeling so good and then to wake up deathly ill, the many surgeries, dying, and how on earth did I miss three whole weeks of my life? Where did the time go? I will never take for granted that I will wake up the next morning and go on with life. I try to always show appreciation for everything Evelyn does for me and just for her sitting next to me or even holding my hand. Every smile she gives to me is important. I don't want to be away from her any length of time and I have even started saying yes *sometimes* when I want to say no, I don't want to go.

TRAVEL

Finally, by the end of May I was finished with all the hospitalizations and surgeries. I asked my doctor for permission to travel by car so my wife and I were driving to Minneapolis to see our children. Well . . . she was driving—she was doing all the driving because I could not drive yet. I think I was in an angry and depressed mood. I had kind of an attitude, some kind of a moody mood so I wasn't talking to her. "That's okay," I suppose she thought and she started playing Dorinda Clark Cole's "Rose of the Gospel" CD. She just played the same song over and over again, "Nobody but God" Now, what did she do that for? I was just staring out the window. I had bought that CD and had given it to my wife because she loves Dorinda. So, she just kept playing it and turning it up just a little bit more. The next thing I knew, I was crying . . . I was crying . . . and I was trying to hide it! I couldn't hide it. I'm crying right now as I think about it. And . . . I reached for one Kleenex, reached for another and . . . I kept crying. If you don't have Dorinda's or Karen's CD's you'd better get those two because they will bless your bones! I just flat out cried, and I cried until I was able to be myself again—to be friendly, and to talk. Those songs reduced me to a YES LORD MOMENT! Those songs put a whipping on me and brought me out of depression into thankfulness. I told Dorinda about it, and I told her that I just wanted to encourage her, and she spoke . . . exhorted me on the things of life, she said she would be praying for me. **"O magnify the LORD with me, and let us exalt his name together."**–Psalms 34:3.

Chapter 8

gaudeamus igitur

MY VOICE RETURNS

Early one morning in May, I woke up coughing and coughed up some phlegm but swallowed it back down. The Lord said to me, "Don't worry, it's coming up again." About five minutes later, I started coughing again and I grabbed a Kleenex and when I spit it out, it was red. I didn't know what it was but I realized that my voice had returned a little stronger than it had been just the day before. I had only been able to whisper but suddenly my voice had returned. I said, "God. Where did that blood come from?" I couldn't taste the blood in my mouth and I decided to try my voice out just to see what would happen. I said, "Thank you, Lord!" Then I said to myself, "I hear my voice!" I said, "Praise You, Lord!" and then I waved my hand and realized that God had caused some blood, phlegm and, maybe, some flesh to get off of my vocal cord and I stayed awake from twelve thirty-five until something after five testifying to myself. I was praising the Lord because I realized that He was yet healing me. Step by step God was putting me back together again.

Well, it might have been a week or a week and a half . . . I don't know. All I know is one day near that time the Lord moved something in my throat. My voice began to clear up . . . I began to talk and I began to hear the power of my voice! I said to my wife, "Listen to this. I can hear my voice coming back!" Oh, I began to try to sing that first Sunday I had been practicing, and I could hear . . . I could sing in baritone. But sometimes my voice would roam off on its own. My wife kept encouraging me to keep singing. So during praise and worship, when everybody was singing, I was trying to sing. And my voice, each Sunday you could hear more of it coming back, and one Sunday, I would hit a little tenor—Praise God! Then one Sunday, while in the pulpit, and my wife said, "Sing! You can sing!" As I sang, the people were startled and stood to their feet while I began to sing that old song, "It's My Desire to Live For Jesus." My wife was crying in amazement—God had answered another prayer. I know many people prayed for me and believed God. But I believe, when that anointed Sister Karen Clark Sheard prayed for me and asked God "To remember what He'd done for her and to do it for me!" I think she put a cap on the prayers. Now, I want to encourage her even now to let God continue to use her—don't sing for the crowd but sing because you love the Lord. His blessings will fall upon you. That is what the Lord told me about her, that if she "Sings for the people to help the people, that He would shower her!" Dorinda, I would encourage her to keep writing those gospel songs. Oh, some of the music you hear today means nothing—it's just fluff stuff. But oh . . . those gospel songs, the promises of God! What He will do and how he will change and bless a person—He can use gospel music to deliver and set people free!

FAMILY AND FRIENDS

After everything that had happened and now that I was closer to recovering, I just wanted to go and see my sons, daughters and granddaughters. I had a hunger for my family; you just don't realize how much they mean to you—you know they mean a lot and you love them but coming back from death and realizing how much they prayed . . . how much effort they had put into coming to see about me . . . seeing their love for me on their faces as they hugged me and kissed me, telling me how much they love me! I realized that they would be missing me if I were not here with them. I told, Evelyn, my wife that the first thing I wanted to do was to go to see my children. Next, I wanted to go back home to Evanston, Illinois to see my old friends there. I had such a hunger to see them—many whom I had grown up near and with—we were all in the choir at Springfield Baptist Church, as children and teenagers, together. Of course, they had called and had been a part of the MIRACLE because of their prayers for me during the illness. In particular, I wanted to see Sister

Jackie Gibbs, Sister Frances Barnett and my little brother, Brother Oliver Ruff. Even he had prayed for me on the telephone. My goddaughter, Mae Hoffman, whom I love like a natural daughter, when I had called her she had prayed for me and the anointing had fallen on her as she spoke in other tongues. As long as I have known her, I've seen her rejoice in the Lord but I have never heard her speak in tongues, but she went for it! She had asked the Lord as well to heal me and she had prayed in the spirit too!

OLD SONGS

Now, I want to go back to the old songs—I have old records. I have Institutional Radio Choir of Brooklyn, New York, songs with Sister Joyce Taylor one of my favorite soloists. I love to hear her sing, "I'm going to stand the storm and it won't be long, I'll anchor by and by." And another song that I enjoyed so much was, "So Good." Listening to those songs would be so good! She would rip those songs. As Bishop Richard "Mr. Clean" White said, "She would sing like you would eat the meat off a bone!" (smile) "She would clean it up." That was one of my favorite singers and also Sister Loretta Oliver and Sister Vernon Oliver Price. With Loretta and Vernon—one would sing with power and the other one would sing with joy. Oh, Loretta would look at you and smile and sing and it would become infectious. Before you knew it, you would be rejoicing with her—Amen! Another favorite is Mr. Jessy Dixon, "I Cannot Fail the Lord!" Oh, that song would just minister to me. I would play it over and over and over again and just cry. "Let Me Live!" That one! I think the correct title is "Christ My Hope." Oh, the early songs of my youth—I still have them and listen to them. I would play them and sing with them because I want to live so God can use me, I want to live and reflect his glory. I'm not interested in getting the glory. I want God to get the glory! I pulled those old songs out, and I played them so much until when my wife is in my car she says, "Oh, Lord!" Every time she gets in my car I'm playing them. These are the songs that brought me through my weak days. When I was laying on my bed of affliction, I couldn't walk, I couldn't eat, I couldn't do anything for myself or by myself. These songs were with me, you know, I Praise God for letting the late Reverend Milton Brunson, and the singers—Estelle Rhinehart, Loretta Oliver, Vernon Oliver Price, Joyce Taylor, Dr. Mattie Moss Clark,

Rubenstein McClure, LaBarbara Whitehead, and Rose Marie Rimson. I admire and enjoy them all! Praise God!

Now, if you're asking why I am writing this and trying to get it written—in that time of recovery, which seemed to take forever for my legs to heal, I have been playing the songs from when I was a young, young man age nineteen or twenty. The Thompson Community Singers, "It Is Well With My Soul," and I heard the powerful voice of my favorite singer—Loretta Oliver, singing "It is Well" while I was in the coma—hallelujah! I came back here knowing that I was free from all of my hurts of the past. I was free—Praise God! Jesus had taken my sins away and I knew it. I didn't have to let the memory of all the hurt and pain come back into the hidden part of my life, He had taken it all away. Now, Satan has tried to bring me back to the past, but I told him what I told Jesus as He ministered to me. "What does it matter?"

"The spirit of a man will sustain his infirmity; But a wounded spirit who can bear?"—Proverbs 18:14.

Chapter 9

laus Deo

POWER OF THE TONGUE

"Death and life are in the power of the tongue: And they that love it shall eat the fruit thereof." –Proverbs 18:21. The Matthew Henry's Commentary says of this verse . . . "Many a one has been his own death by a foul tongue, or the death of others by a false tongue; and, on the contrary, many a one has saved his life by a prudent gentle tongue, and saved the lives of

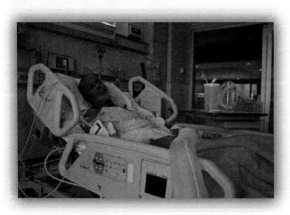

others by intercession for them." My life was saved only by the intercession of others along with the grace and mercy of God.

I have seen angels many times during the years of ministry here in Rapid City but it is really something that during my hospital stay, I never saw a one. I realized that they were on duty, but the Lord Himself was keeping me company. He was there all the time. Many times sitting in the room talking to me and sometimes taking me out of the room and showing me things. One thing for sure, I have learned that the spirit world is much closer to our world than we think. Those first few days recovering, I felt like I could see into both worlds. The Lord would talk to me and explain things to me. I remember waking one day and telling my wife, "I AM FREE!" Things that had bothered me, the Lord took them and my spirit got healed from so many wounds. Just being in the presence of the Lord set me free set me free and I am free indeed.

THE DEATH OF OUR SON

I want to thank the Lord that my story is not exactly like that of Job but I can definitely feel some similarities. There are song lyrics about Job's experience that go something like this, "Job was sick so long until the flesh fell from him bones. His wife, family and children—everything that he had was gone. Job waited on the Lord so tell me why can't I?" I have so much to be thankful for that God has not called me to be a twenty-first-century Job! I am so thankful that I do have a wife and children who loves me very dearly. I simply praise the Lord for His everlasting goodness to me and my family. However, almost two years after my grave sickness and death, our oldest son, Thomas Christopher, died. He suffered a brain aneurysm and was critically ill, in a coma and on life support for four long weeks before going into eternity.

Because the Lord had healed me and raised me from the dead, I had not expected that Thomas would die. Yes, I saw him lying in that intensive care unit, swollen with all kinds of tubes in his head and body. He lay there helpless and unmoving day after day but we kept waiting for some semblance of hope to show up. It did. He seemed to have improved just at the end but instead of his being better—he died. Right there in our presence on Saturday, February 2, 2008 he passed away into eternity. His upcoming birthday was just nine days away—he was almost forty-two years old. It was a dark, cold and dismal day and we all stumbled away—mostly in disbelief of what had just happened. Lots of tears. Lots of shock while yet facing reality. Thomas's friends were devastated and seemed to believe that they could somehow bring him back from that place of finality that he had just slipped away to.

The enemy said to me, "Now, what are you going to do?" My answer was this, "The Lord has my life, and I have an eternal YES down in my soul." I said, "Yes, Lord . . . even to Thomas's dying. The Will of the Lord be done." You see, I have given my life totally over to the Lord. He owns me and I often say I have come too far with Him. I love Him so much and I trust Him with all of me and mine. I will never forget stumbling away from his deathbed crying yet saying, "Yes, Lord!" He couldn't talk to us but we believe he knew we were with him and we saw a tear roll down his face as his close friends, along with family, surrounded him. He had often said that Scott and I were his favorite singers so I began to sing, "Jesus Loves Me" and "Great Is Thy Faithfulness." Scott joined in with me and then my wife along with others in the room began to sing to him. We gave Thomas permission to leave as we continued and as long as we sang, he stayed with us with an increased (instead of a decreased) heartbeat. When we stopped singing, Thomas left us and we know that he is in good hands in the care of the Lord. I have determined to give Christ my all and that is what I have done!

At Thomas's funeral we were very happily surprised that so many people came to share in the farewell. Really! Friends and relatives came on such a short notice (he left on Saturday and the service was held on the following Wednesday) and they came from great distances as well as from all over the Twin Cities areas. Evelyn and I had gotten the opportunity to bond with many of Thomas's friends while we all sat and shared together during the three and one half weeks of his illness and critical care. It was so encouraging to see that Thomas had touched the lives of so many people with whom he had known over the years. I preached the Eulogy and the subject was "Prodigal Son, Come Home!" During the message, I gave the opportunity for acceptance of and/or of return to a relationship with the Lord. It was so inspirational to see hundreds of people stand to receive prayer as a response to the invitation.

It was a cold and wintry day and the snow was very deep as we trudged through the cemetery to Thomas's final resting place. The loved ones of Thomas crowded around the casket and bier and as the final words were spoken over him, you could hear the soft cries of anguish and loss from his family and friends. Glancing back as we were being driven away from the grave site, many of Thomas's friends were still standing there numb with disbelief and some were holding onto and touching the casket. The loss of a son and dear friend was felt very deeply by many and no amount of forewarning could have prepared us for the empty space that was now a very real part of our lives. Yet and still I will always bow to the will of the Lord. Sometimes, it might cause me to feel anguish and to struggle but I KNOW that whatever the Lord does is good.

Thomas had often mentioned that "I know I'm going before you, mom and dad! I want to because I just couldn't take it if you left me here!

Dad, that's why I was so upset when you were ill because I knew I was suppose to go first." He had often spoken to his brother Scott having this same conversation however he had not ever mentioned it to his youngest brother Loren. Even though we'd had this conversation his leaving still took many of the family members by dismay and surprise. Scott and Loren have deeply grieved Thomas's passing and, after two years of fitful wrestling with their loss, are beginning the process of acceptance. Acceptance of their loss means accepting the Lord's will. Accepting the Lord's will then can make the difference in how they go forward in this life! My wife had sensed, a long time before Thomas' passing, that he would leave us early.

When it finally came right down to it, she seemed to be the only one who was truly prepared for it. Even though this was the child that first opened her womb—her firstborn son—she seemed not to be gripped by anguish at the loss but rather by God's peace, love mercy and grace.

WHAT DOES JESUS LOOK LIKE?

When I told my family that I had seen Jesus, my brother asked me, "What does He look like? What color is He?" I can't tell you what color He is or what color I was when I was with Him, Nor can I tell you what His features look like. All I know is I saw Him and He talked with me. Bless the Lord! The Lord always brought peace with Him—He is truly the Prince of Peace!

MIRACLE WORKING GOD

The story is not complete as there are so many more wonderful and miraculous events that took place during the whole ordeal. Now that it has been nearly four years, I have continued to regain my strength on a daily basis. There is a former physician who is a part of a group of men who gather for coffee a few times a week. He is quick to remind me that, "You are a ticking time bomb just waiting to happen!" You see, he cannot believe the MIRACLE that God worked in my life—he's used to dealing in the natural but not in the spiritual matters of life. God has taught me, especially in what has happened, that in life we must handle both the natural as well as the spiritual issues that confront us!

Because all of my organs were shut down and frozen for the surgery the doctors were especially concerned about my kidneys continuing to function properly. In fact, the kidney specialist really expected that I would become a permanent kidney dialysis patient. In 2009, I've had to undergo several tests and two biopsy's of 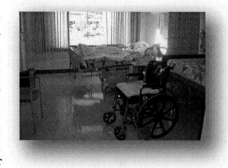 my kidney to determine its ability. Also, I've just had my annual physical examination and I am in top notch condition—in every aspect. AND, NO, I am not a candidate for kidney dialysis. You want to tell me about God? I'll tell you, He is a MIRACLE WORKING GOD! I have determined to and have given Christ my all! I will serve Him for the rest of my life and I will serve Him in holiness and sanctification! What about you?

The Rehabilitation Hospital Room. That was a temporary setting—THANK GOD!

That Saturday morning when I was in such pain, the one thing I didn't have to rush and do was to ask the Lord to forgive me because I knew that I was already forgiven. Instead, I praised Him. I figured that if I was going to go out . . . I was going to go out PRAISING **Him!** I had peace with the Lord and I have peace with the Lord now. He's a good God! I wasn't pleading for my life because I felt like I was going to die right there. That's when the Holy Ghost began to speak forth out of my belly. The scripture says that, "Out of your belly shall flow rivers of living water." Well, those living waters flowed out of my belly and I am here today still testifying about the great goodness of the Lord.

Even when I died, the Lord brought me back. When the enemy tried to take me out of here, God said, "No! Not yet! Not done with him!" When I think of His goodness to me, I want to bless Him and thank Him!

"For I reckon that the sufferings of this present time are not worthy to be compared with the glory which shall be revealed in us."–Romans 8:18

"Whoso findeth a wife findeth a good thing, and obtaineth favour of the LORD." —Proverbs 18:22

His Story
He is Alive Again!

Mrs. Evelyn A. Kelly

Chapter 10

Sans souci

REFLECTIONS

Tuesday, October 6, 2009. It had to be God's timing that caused us to plan this trip to Kauai, Hawaii in March of this year for travel in October to celebrate our forty-fifth wedding anniversary on Saturday, October 10. Only God would have known that we would escape the very first Rapid City, South Dakota snow storm and freezing weather of the season. I was sitting on a lounge chair, in my swim suit, watching my husband as he was walking toward me. The horrific scars from his ordeal, nearly four years ago, were blatantly evident showing below the hem of his swim trunks. He said, "My poor legs!" and I responded, "I'm so grateful that you have them!" When you know the rest of the story, you will agree with me to shout out "Glory to God in the highest!" for the wonderful things that He has done!

In September of 2005, my husband had come down with a flu type of condition that just would not go away. In late August, we had eaten at a local restaurant in Rapid City, South Dakota where we live. Later on, through the news media, we learned that a number of people who had eaten at that same restaurant over the summer months had become severely ill one person had even died, even the mayor of our city, Mayor Jim Shaw, had not only been hospitalized but had also had to go undergo open heart surgery. The Legionnaires Disease was the diagnosis and the cause was air spores breathed in from the display water fountain at that restaurant. We didn't connect the fact that his flu symptoms could have been connected to our luncheon visit to that local establishment, however, there seemed to be no antibiotic prescribed that could or would completely eliminate my husband's flu-like symptoms. He then began to get large-peeling splotches on his chest and back and his doctor's only remedy was to change him from one antibiotic to another thinking he was allergic to the current one. The last medication prescribed was Levaquin and I would, later, become very suspicious that this was one that strongly contributed to my husband's severe medical condition. Also, probably & possibly, contributing was the fact that he had been diagnosed with hypertension when he was in his late thirties and had been on high blood pressure medication for a number of years. His blood pressure was controlled by medication but, I guess it's probable that some damage could have occurred to his physical being. Who knows all the why's and what for's of any given situation??? Well, let's continue.

In October of 2005, our church sent us on a seven-night cruise as an anniversary gift. The MSC Opera Cruise Ship departed from Venice, Italy and docked in Greece, Turkey and Croatia. Often, my mind just imagines and wonders what if he had gotten ill while we were on that cruise ship so far away from home? I'm certain that he would  not be with us, in the land of the living, today. We were on that ship not knowing or imagining that in three and a half short months, my husband would be deathly ill and on an operating table, frozen and helpless, as the medical team would be feverishly fighting to save his life. Even so, just a few days prior to January 28, 2006, he had just returned from preaching a revival service in Jonesboro, Arkansas. He had traveled alone, and later told me, that he had experienced trouble breathing the night before his return trip home. He was so miserable until he had to sit up, in the recliner chair, and sleep the best he could in an upright position. Little did he know or suspect the impending danger that he was to face in a few short days. When I think of this, I think "Oh, my God!" my husband was in imminent danger of passing away and none of us knew nor suspected what was just around the corner of life.

Chapter 11

nolens volens

IS IT A HEART ATTACK?

Saturday, January 28, 2006. On that fateful Saturday morning, he remembers awaking with pain in his chest and he does not recall that he'd been up for a short while before everything happened. He and I had a short business meeting discussing the appointment of the new youth pastor. I had been waiting, for a couple of weeks, upon his decision about the selection of the new youth pastor for our church and, after a short discussion he gave his approval that early morning. I had a busy day planned ahead of me and, had already gone back to bed once which had delayed my getting out of the house earlier that morning. The fourth Saturday of January is a traditional day for our church's Women's Department and is our "kick-off fellowship" event for the year. Also scheduled on that same day, was an all day recording session at the studio that I owned. I needed to be up and out of the house at least by eight thirty and it was now closer to nine o'clock and I had further delayed myself by deciding on a last minute shampoo while I was in the shower. Finally, just as I was close to being ready to run out the door, my hair was done and I was dressed except for putting on my suit jacket was when my husband walked into my room, hand on his chest with a startled look on his face, and said "I just took my blood pressure medicine and my chest hurts!" Isn't God wonderful? I appreciate the little things because they can sometimes make all the difference between life and death and the fact that he had just taken his high blood pressure medicine made a big difference in the things that were to happen next, in my opinion. I think it bought us some time and we, not knowing it at the time, truly needed time on our side.

Thank God that I was still at home at nine o'clock that morning. I appreciate the little things because they can sometimes make all the difference between life and death! I should've left home at least by eight thirty but I was still at home when the pain struck at around nine o'clock! Well, I jumped into gear and my immediate response was "Sit down, I'm going to call 911!" and his immediate response was "No, don't call, I'm going to be okay!" as he was still holding his chest with that surprised look on his face. It had to be the LORD that caused me to dial our Assistant Pastor first and to ask him to "come quickly, it looks like bishop might be having a heart attack!" Having never ever had to make a 911 call before, I had no idea that I would be required to stay on the phone with the operator the entire time until the ambulance arrived at our door. If I had not called Elder Carr, first, before calling 911. I would not have been able to call him and he would not have been there to ride in the ambulance with Bishop. I appreciate the little things . . . and it gave me comfort to know that Elder Carr was on the way to the house while we were in the midst of this unknown ordeal.

I thought that he should take an aspirin but I didn't know where they were so I had begun a slight tailspin wondering where to look for the aspirin. He said, "I have some in my bathroom" and got up and walked the short distance down the hall, from the master bedroom, and took the aspirin. Next, as 911 were answering the call, my husband sat down in his recliner chair and the pains were swifter and worsening by the moment. It kind of looked as if someone was, literally, punching him in the chest, ribs and stomach as he would grimace and grab himself in those places. He locked eyes with me and said, "Ev . . . I love you!" PAIN—grimace, scream, and grab! "LORD, You know I love you!" PAIN—grimace, scream, and grab! Then, he began to speak in an unknown tongue that was so beautiful and so vastly different than any either of us had ever heard. I've never heard any words so beautiful yet so demanding before or since. It appeared that the Holy Ghost was not only speaking to the Father on my husband's behalf but was actively interceding for this godly man's life. WOW!

The 911 operator was asking me to describe his pain and his reaction to the pain even while she was giving me instructions over the phone. At the same instance that she was telling me not to leave him alone for a moment, she was telling me that I would need to be able to open the front door for the paramedics. She was telling me to make sure that any animals in the home were put away so that they would not interfere with the paramedics work when they arrived. She was repeatedly asking me what my husband was saying every time she heard his voice. I told her it all, including the fact that he was speaking in an unknown tongue empowered by the Holy Ghost. I appreciate the little things . . . because they just might develop into something big! This little thing, this other tongue thing, was a big thing . . . and we both think that it made the complete difference between life and death that day. Those long moments (seemed like an eternity) while I was on the line with 911 became an actual procedure as he would do the same thing over and over again he locked eyes with me and said, "Ev, I love you!" PAIN—grimace, screech, and grab! "LORD, You know I love you!" PAIN—grimace, shriek, and grab! Then, he began to speak in that unknown tongue and the 911 operator would say again, "What is he saying?" "Describe his pain!" The severe pain in his upper chest, his abdomen and his lower middle back rocked him so much until there were times that his body would literally almost get tossed out of the recliner, as he struggled with the intensifying bouts of pain. I would brace my knee against him to keep him from rolling over the arm of the chair and onto the floor and at the same time, the 911 operator was still barreling questions at me as I held the cordless phone with one hand and braced my knee against the recliner to block a fall.

It was and is so amazing, the strength that God gave my husband to endure and live throughout this ordeal. When the paramedics arrived, they were not able to get the stretcher all the way into the bedroom because the hallway was too narrow. In the midst of all that pain, my husband was alert enough to suggest that he could get up from the recliner and walk over to the stretcher . . . I asked them if that was all right and they seemed to breathe a sigh of relief at the suggestion. My husband then got up out of his chair, with just a little help from one of the paramedics, and walked the few short feet from the bedroom to the waiting stretcher there in the hallway. Just as they rolled my husband outside on the stretcher, Elder Carr had arrived and was able to get into the ambulance and ride with him to the hospital. The way my husband describes the ride, besides being (or seeming) much slower than most ambulance rides that we see whisking through town when it is "the other person", the Holy Ghost kept right on speaking throughout the entire ride. He, now, laughingly tells it that he said to the Lord "They're going to think I'm crazy and take me to the wrong hospital!" You see, the Psychiatric Hospital is closer to our home than the Rapid City Regional Hospital and he figured that they, not understanding that the Holy Ghost was at work, would think he needed a different kind of hospital (smile). He remembers that almost the moment that he was rolled into the Emergency Room, the unknown tongues ceased as he was now in the care of the medical team.

After examination by the Emergency Room physicians, it was diagnosed that he was having an aneurysm of the thoracic aorta and would require immediate surgery in order to, possibly, save his life. Dr. Gordon explained the severity of this situation and that not knowing how long the tear in the aorta was that this surgery would be both in depth and aggressive and said, "We can't promise that he will live!" Further, they would need to freeze his body in order that other organs would not place a demand for blood flow or any other need. Dr. Gordon mentioned, with a sigh of relief, that the "flap" that connects the aorta to the heart had not blown or burst and that was a good thing. Bishop Kelly was wheeled down the hallway and into the Operating Room within three hours of the first onset of severe pain, for what would be a true life and death experience. Multiple times over . . . death and life; life and death; death and life; and so on.

Dr. Robert Gordon later explained that because of the location of the first onset of pain that really, my husband should've died immediately from a massive brain stroke. He said, "It should have traveled up both sides of his neck, up the Carotid Arteries, and resulted in a massive brain stroke. I don't understand why it didn't!" Next, had the tear of the aneurysm torn through both the inner and outer linings Lorenzo would have died on the spot! It was God and Him alone who held my husband's life in the palm of His wonderful hands until such a time as help was available. God, all along, knew that He would get the glory and praise for what He would do and we, continuously, give Him praise, honor and thanksgiving—even now, nearly four years later!

For the next ten hours my husband's life hung in the balance as it was determined that the aortic tear traveled all the way from the valve flap down to just above the renal arteries. Surgery required replacement of eighteen inches of the ascending aorta with resuspension of the aortic valve, replacement of the transverse arch, with reimplantation of the innominate left carotid and subclavian arteries, as well as replacement of the upper descending aorta. The first surgery lasted for ten hours during which time Bishop Kelly died (code blue) five times on the operating table.

As mentioned before, they had frozen him for the surgery lowering his body temperature down to about thirty-six degrees. In the process of the surgery, at some point, his body temperature dropped dramatically down to between fourteen and seventeen degrees. With all the code blues that the surgical team was dealing with along with the thoracic aorta surgery, in their attempts to save his life, they began to try to get his blood to warm up again. Too much was happening too fast and a decision was made to place heat in the room over and around his body to help to return his normal body temperature. Simply, they were using a warmer unit that is used on premature babies but, in the midst of everything else, someone forgot to pay attention to how long the heat was left pouring over his body. When they realized anything, Bishop Lorenzo L. Kelly had, inadvertently, sustained severe (what would later be diagnosed as) fourth degree burns to the front of both legs. There was not time to deal with this, right then, because they were still anxiously working to save this man's life . . . I believe it was mandated by the Lord, Himself. Death at this time, and for this cause, was absolutely not acceptable to the Lord and, therefore, He pushed the surgical team to do more than they'd ever done before in a situation like this. Seems to me, that if the aneurysm didn't kill him, then the fourth degree burns should have helped to finish him off but no, not yet! This was not God's appointed time of death and there was a fight going on over this wonderful man's life and who knew what the outcome would be?? Certainly not the doctors! Certainly not me! Certainly, not the hundreds of people that were already praying and interceding all across America for this man's life. Only

God! I was so very surprised to get a phone call that afternoon, from Bishop John H. Sheard, asking about what was going on? It is such a small world! We had just told our children and our church family that my husband was very ill but a friend of our sons, in Minneapolis, had grown up in Sheard's church and had called to tell his grandma who had informed her pastor, Bishop Sheard.

Dr. Gordon had come into the Davies Family Waiting Room a number of times to, briefly, speak with me and to give updates about my husband's condition.

He continued to acknowledge that he could not guarantee anything but that everything was "in the hands of the Man upstairs!" He further stated that only 10% of people, in this emergent condition, ever get off the table and only a small of percentage of those are able to go on and live normal lives. He said, "So far, he's in the ten percent!" Well, at the conclusion of the first (ten hour) surgery while they were attempting to stitch him they were not able to do so because, as Dr. Gordon explained, "He would start dying again because of the extreme swelling caused by excess fluids!" In their determination that this man would live, they were forced to leave his chest (sternum) open for three days leaving him in a cellophane type wrapping.

Chapter 12

locus in quo

OUR CHILDREN ARRIVE

Literally, we have hundreds of God-given children who lovingly and respectfully call us Mom and Dad. Our natural-born children have *always* had to share us with others who needed to know what it was like to have loving parents. I don't know if they resented it or not because that was the way it always was—it's just our way of life. Always!

Early that Saturday morning, they had gotten themselves together to take the highway home and within a couple of hours they were driving this way. At that time, all three of our sons lived in the Minneapolis area but since then our firstborn son, Thomas, has passed away in 2008. Thomas always expected  that he would leave us here on this earth so every time one of his parents became ill, he would get completely hysterical. It was kind of funny because he was so big ("Kong!") and he had the appearance of one who could take anything and who could take on any one (smile). Well, that was probably true in any other situation except for either of his parents becoming ill. So, as usual, he responded unashamedly hysterical—screaming and howling over the phone, wanting to speak to him just before his dad was wheeled down the hall for the first of many operations. When my husband answered the phone, he asked Thomas, "Why are you crying? I'm the one in pain!" Hearing his father's voice, Thomas was able to calm down just a little. The weather was icy, sleety and snowy in places, as they traveled those endless miles on the long road home. They arrived around midnight all three car load after about nine hours on the road—Thomas, Scott, Loren, Shelly, Cara, Mikaela, Aleah, Jahnaya, Beatriz (three weeks old); as well as our god-daughter, Leona Derden, and her husband, William. Their dad had been out of surgery for a couple of hours, and they kept the overnight vigil waiting and praying for their beloved father.

They had sent me home to rest a while so I was not present for these events but while they were holding watch in the Davies Family Waiting Room they were told, "Come now to see him, if you want to see him alive!" About two to three hours after he was rolled into recovery, it was discovered that there was a bleeding leakage in the chest and determined that he would need to be returned to the operating room immediately. I heard that this was a very emotional time and that our sons, Thomas in particular, wept and wailed for the life of their father. So, about four hours after the first surgery ended, the second surgery began and lasted for six more hours.

THE SECOND SURGERY

Sunday Morning, January 29, 2006. Finally, at about 8:00 AM on Sunday morning, they had found the source of and had stopped the bleeding but could not guarantee that it wouldn't occur again. The excess fluids, in his body, were caused by the amount of fluids that needed to be pumped into him to help to avoid infections to the new graft (aorta) site from the burn sites below. We were allowed brief moments to visit him there in the surgical intensive care ward, and you could see his heart, thumping, through the cellophane wrapping over his chest. It would be necessary, as soon as possible, to get him started on a twenty-four hour dialysis treatment in order to drain off as much fluid as possible from his massively-swollen body. His body was swollen beyond what it could stand so dialysis was scheduled to begin later that day and run for twenty-four hours straight. You must understand here that due to his body being frozen, none of his organs were working and everything would have to be reactivated again, at some point. He was heavily sedated with large doses of narcotics, to keep him under, and he was to remain that way for days or weeks, depending upon recovery, so that any other emergency surgical procedures would not need to be delayed. Additionally, he was placed on total life support with no guarantees. No guarantees, "It's all up to the Man upstairs!"

When we asked about the burns on my husband's legs, the nurse's reaction was "how did you know? We told her that we had been informed just after it happened on the day before and she had kind of a surprised look on her face. This left us with a feeling of trepidation because, it seemed as if, there was something that they felt a need to be secretive about. Finally, they said, "Oh, don't worry, it's just like a slight sunburn or no more than second degree burns, if that." The nurse further explained that the burns would be attended to on Tuesday during the next surgery to close the sternum and everything should be quite all right. It was later explained to me that the burns occurred with flames, deep burns that would require skin grafting. The physiological consequences of the burns were that my husband would require massive amounts of nutritive fluids which would support all of his vital body systems. Dr. Gordon made sure to continue to reinforce to us that, "He's not out of the woods yet—if he lives, it could take up to six months for his recovery. He could be hospitalized for six months or more."

Sons and daughters, who had come through the ministry of Faith Temple Church in Rapid City, began to return home to see about "dad!" The first to arrive, that Sunday afternoon, were Colonel/Elder Herman Hicks and Elder Ezzard Luke from Wichita, Kansas. Oh, the prayers and interceders were starting to form watch out, the Kingdom of God was just about to get bombarded through faith and prayer!

The Rapid City Journal made contact with me wanting to print a news release about my husband's condition. I had been warned by Elder Cliette that this would happen but I was still surprised especially when her questions seemed to be interrogative. God gave me the wisdom to get in touch with the hospital's Public Relation Department which proved to be my protection and connection for any news information that was to be printed about my husband's condition. Nothing could be published without my written approval and that was the way it was for the entire time.

Chapter 13

in extremis

AT THE POINT OF DEATH

Monday, January 30, 2006. On Monday, seeing him laying there unconscious like that . . . so helpless, eyes staring aimlessly if they were open . . . body grossly swollen looking like a big rubber doll . . . tubes coming from his mouth, his nose, his arms, his chest and his abdomen. We were allowed brief visits with no more than two people at a time and the Davies Family Waiting Room was continuing to fill up with friends, strangers and acquaintances who wanted to be of any support that they could be to our family. That was awesome! Oh, and by now, the phone was beginning to ring literally, off the hook, not just the phone but all the phones. The waiting room phones, the house phone, the church phone, the cell phones, friend's phones and so on. People were calling to express their care and concern and they were praying . . . watch out, the Kingdom of God was just about to get bombarded through faith and prayer! Elder Matthew Mock flew in from Wisconsin. Missionary Sharon Colquitt flew in from Atlanta, Georgia. The late Bishop G. E. Patterson, who was then the Presiding Bishop of the Church of God in Christ, called me to express his support through prayer and intercession. When I expressed the shock that he would take the time to call about my husband's condition, he exclaimed, "As nice as you and Bishop Kelly have been to Louise and me, of course, I must let you know our concern!" He then proceeded to recall some of those things including the beautiful crocheted blanket that my husband had made for them.

Many pastors of our city who did not have a relationship with my husband or me, nor do they yet today, called or stopped by to pray. I heard that most pulpits in our town were mentioning, calling out, my husband's name in prayer from one Sunday to another. My, my, my! The Kingdom of God was getting bombarded through faith and prayer! I found that it was impossible to answer all the calls even with family there to help and God gave me the thought to set up one of the phones as an update line. Each morning, then, I began to leave messages on one specific phone detailing the prayer needs for the day. Each day had its own crisis that we had to contend with and I knew we could not do it alone if this wonderful man's life was going to be returned to him and to us! My, my, my! The Kingdom of God was just about to get bombarded through faith and prayer! Many people would call, listen to the message and just go into prayer for us—they knew that we could not return so many calls so they would say, "You don't need to call me back, I know you're busy, just wanted you to know that we are praying!"

At the same time, I became aware of several strange people who we did not know but wanted to come in a stand over my husband's bed in prayer. My spiritual antenna was sensing dangerous visitations sent in by Satan to cause irreparable harm to my husband's ever so critical situation. After a second incident, with persons just walking into the surgical intensive care room where my husband lay, helplessly, between life and death; I demanded that the nurses screen all visitors and to not allow anyone inside, whose name was not on the list.

The first twenty-four hours of dialysis was done and they had been able to pull off quite a bit of the fluid that was loaded into my husband's body but they would need to start it up again in just a few hours. In order for his body to endure the closure of the sternum, he still needed more fluids removed from his body, and other crucial situations were occurring that they did not, always, explain to us, due to the urgency of the moment. There were times that we would go to the surgical intensive care ward for our scheduled fifteen-minute visit and we would be sent away and told, "Come back in thirty minutes or an hour!" When we would return, they would tell us the same thing and send us away again. Later, in reading the medical records, I was to learn that he even coded blue right in the middle of some procedure or another right there in his room. The records would indicate "We did not have time to contact the family for a signature but had to act hastily to get the present situation under control!"

THE THIRD SURGERY

Tuesday, January 31, 2006. On that afternoon, Bishop Kelly had surgery, again, for next two procedures. First, the skin graft/debriding operation to the burn sites on the front of both legs; second, to close up the sternum (stitch up the chest). Preceding the time of surgery, on that day, as friends and loved ones came to visit and spend time with us in the Davies Family Waiting Room we had a number of large circle prayer sessions. I knew we were on the right track when there was a complaint about our praying in this fashion by someone else in the same room. The waiting room attendant explained that "your praying is frightening to her so could you move your group to a different room?" I responded to her, very strongly and in no uncertain terms, that "we are not about to stop praying neither will we relocate for prayer! If someone is uncomfortable then they should move, not us!" I was sure that Satan was planning to use the next time of surgery as an opportunity to bring about my husband's death and I was determined that, since we had made it thus far, that certainly we could make it to the end . . . by the grace and help of the Lord! We stood in a circle, holding hands, and prayed every hour on the hour—as more people showed up, the circle kept getting bigger and bigger. My, my, my! The Kingdom of God was just getting bombarded through faith and prayer! My husband came through that operation successfully and I was, continuously, reminded that we weren't being promised anything as to his recovery. "It's up to the Man upstairs," Dr. Gordon would always repeat this. It was kind of his disclaimer that if things went the wrong, he was doing all that he could do and, he realized, that the rest was up to the Lord!

Chapter 14

suo jure

THEY CAME, THEY CONQUERED

Elder Jimmy Pierce drove in from the Tacoma, Washington area. Bishop and Mrs. James Austin of Chicago, Illinois flew in. Our god daughter, Mae Hoffman, flew in from Chicago, Illinois. Of course, our sons and families were still here: Thomas; Scott & Shelly (Mikaela, Aleah & Jahnaya); and Loren & Cara (and one month old, Beatriz); and, Leona & William Derden.

Elder and Mrs. Adrian Rodgers flew here from Jonesboro, Arkansas. Since the first surgery ended on that previous Saturday evening, Bishop Kelly had laid, helplessly, in the surgical intensive care ward, in a deep coma and on total life support. The machines were all around him and he was hooked up to all kinds of tubing. It's hard, even now, to fathom just how many times I was asked to sign a new paper approving a new surgical procedure. He was so very ill until he could not be moved from his room. They would bring the surgery team to his bedside to perform whichever was the "necessary" one or three for the day! He had no idea what all was happening to him and, most of the time, I felt so guilty for putting

Left Knee & Leg Burns ↑
& Right Leg burns ↓

him through more and more cuttings and surgical procedures. Of course, I had no idea whether after all of this if he would live or die. I thought, at times, that he would be very upset with me for letting them do all of this to him. The surgery was successful, the sternum was closed. More tubes. The burn wounds had been scraped (debrided, pronounced, debreeded) which means they had to go down up under where the nerve endings had been burned off and remove the dead layers of skin. OUCH! This would be the first of several surgical procedures to those precious legs so this was just the beginning! The wrapping around the legs was supposed to be removed within forty-eight hours for examination and redressing and an accurate burn depth diagnosis. As yet, they had not confessed that their accidental burning of his legs was at least fourth degree burns—that would be noted in the medical records at a later time.

Wednesday, February 1, 2006. I finally got around to returning a phone call from our god daughter, Sherri Lewis on Wednesday morning to learn that she wanted to set a date from Bishop to come and perform a renewal of vows ceremony later in the year. I told her what was happening and she said, "Oh, my! We'll be praying!" Well, they did a lot more than pray. They immediately boarded an airplane in Charleston, North Carolina, and arrived in Rapid City by midnight that same day. Wow! You see what I mean? These two, Elder Joseph Lewis and Evangelist Cherri Lewis, were also founding members of our church and they call us mom and dad. So much love, so many prayers standing in the gap for this wonderful man's life. What you going to do, Lord?

Chapter 15

in medias res

SO MUCH SUFFERING

Because of the extreme bodily swelling, it seemed that it was very easy for sores to develop on Lorenzo's body. His left shoulder had a large sore where the tape, holding down some of the tubes coming from the chest, had pulled the skin off. There was a sore just above the upper lip, below the nose, that spread more and more each day, it seemed. This was from the tubing that was in his nostril down into his stomach. Eventually, it burst open on the upper lip and for some reason the nursing staff didn't know how to treat the sores. I insisted on them putting a salve or Vaseline on these areas often and scabs were forming but the sores would break open again. I brought in a healing concoction that I use at home with honey and Vaseline mixed together and, in time, the sores began to heal.

His skin had turned extremely dark and he lay, in one spot just stretched out and swollen, and in so much unknown pain because of the deep pain medication that he was on. If you turned his head to a different position, it just automatically returned to where it had been. Eventually, he developed a sore on the back of his head from it lying in the one position—to this day, you can see the bald circle where his hair was lost. It has never grown back and that's okay with me as I'd rather have him with me and I treasure that little bald spot on the back of his head.

Saturday, February 4, 2006. Dr. Shultz, the Plastic Surgeon assigned to care for my husband's legs, had been too busy to take care of that forty-eight-hour change of dressing which should have occurred on Thursday. At twelve-thirty on Saturday, I demanded that "Dr. Shultz or somebody better get here and get this done . . . it has been almost seventy-two hours and nothing has been done about my husband's legs." The poor nurse exclaimed in weariness that she had been calling the doctor's office and they were getting irritated with her for insisting upon his visit to my husband's critical legs situation. The doctor finally arrived at about three o'clock that afternoon and unwrapped those precious legs . . . my camera was flashing. My God! What a surprise to see the depth of injury caused by someone's oversight and this was in no way related to the aneurysm of the thoracic aorta. IN NO WAY RELATED!

As if all of this wasn't bad enough, the next surprise was that Lorenzo contracted the MRSA Staph Infection which, at that particular time, approximately ninety thousand people in America had died from. It is a bacterial staph infection that comes from within the hospital institution as a patient is inside the facility. Each visitor was required to cap, gown, face mask, wash hands and glove up before entering his room on the surgical intensive care ward. It was amazing, to me, knowing that such a serious infection which comes from within the hospital, that some of the staff who had to perform medical procedures on my husband did not put on gloves nor did they do any of the things mentioned above. Early one morning, after I had slept in the rocking chair in his room to watch him, they needed to get a new x-ray of his chest area. He still could not be transported—he was still too critical—so they brought everything needed with them. There were two men and a lady in hospital technician attire. They just entered his room, handled him to perform the procedure and then they left. This is how patients get infected because it is passed from patient to patient by the staff that travels around the hospital. I saw this with my own eyes and wondered, again, at what length Satan would go to in order to kill my husband.

There is yet more that he endured and this was just the first phase of his hospital stay. For the most part, the nurses, doctors and the entire medical teams were awesome and worked tirelessly to make sure that my husband was taken care of in every way possible. There was one nurse, however, that seemed to be on assignment to bring harm to him and we were able to pick up on it by noticing Lorenzo's body language when she was around nursing him. She seemed ever so sweet but, even though he could not speak to us, we could tell that he did not feel safe whenever she was in his room. We had begun, earlier in this whole experience, to assign family and friends who would stay in the hospital, around the clock, to be present in case of any new event or emergency. I had been the person on duty during that particular day and had made a quick trip home. Scott was the family member on duty that evening and he called me, at home, and said, "Mom, I think we'd better get this nurse removed from Dad's care. He's been lying so still for hours, as if he was sleeping, but now that she's off duty he's starting to seem more alert again." As nice as this nurse had seemed, I too had noticed and felt that something wasn't quite right, there. Early the next day, oh about seven in the morning, I asked to speak with the supervisor of the nurses and she granted me a meeting in her office. I told her that we didn't know what was wrong or why my husband felt unsafe with that particular nurse but we wanted her removed from his care. I asked her to please ask her not to enter his room at all. The supervisor told me that this particular nurse was working a lot of days on, with minimal days off, and was actually requesting Lorenzo as her patient. He really started to improve after this but most of his organs and bodily functions had not returned to normal function.

By this time, he had so many different physicians, specialists who all worked together as a team to get him well. Dr. Reyno told me that Lorenzo was showing signs of an infection coming up from the burned legs which could overtake the thoracic aorta graft—they were extremely concerned about this. I signed my approval for a surgical procedure where they would cut him from the left nipple to about one-fourth of the way around his back. This was so that they could wash out the new infection that was forming. They already had about six units setting on the floor, at the foot of the bed, that several tubes connected from his chest area drained the infectious fluids out from his body. This was a thick, yellowish-orange-tan type of colors and each unit (stood about a foot tall and, maybe, eight inches wide) slowly filled day by day.

He was on the Ventilator with a breathing tube down his throat some days past the recommended time. They explained to me that if this tubing was left in for too long then it could cause irreparable damage to his vocal cords. They needed to remove the breathing tube and perform a tracheotomy on him as soon as possible. I signed the approval form but several days later they still had not performed that procedure. One day, I was at my studio office (Everose Productions Recording Studio, Inc.) and I called to check on my husband. They said that he had pulled the tubing out of his nose, which is how they were giving him some of the necessary medications, and this was the second time he had pulled it out. They wanted my permission, over the phone, to reinsert it through his nostril down into his stomach again. I said, "No!" and the nurse desperately replied, "But, Mrs. Kelly, how will we give him his medications?" I determinedly replied, "With all the technology and know-how that you all have, you'd better figure out something but don't you dare reinsert that tubing. Don't touch him until I get there and I'm on the way!" You know, I'm just a five minute drive down the street so I ran out of my office and got back over to the hospital. By the time I parked and ran into the hospital, down the hall, and into the surgical intensive care ward it couldn't have been more than fifteen minutes. However, by the time I ran through those big swinging doors, the nurse assured me that they had figured out another way to administer the medications. I assured her, "I thought you could!"

Two weeks after the initial surgery, our son Thomas and I were in his room on a Sunday morning and we were trying to talk with him. I asked him, "Honey, do you want to stay with us or do you want to go to be with the Lord?" I asked him a couple of times and thought, that somehow, he understood what I was saying. At one point, when I repeated it, we noticed a slight moving up and down of his head and I, excitedly, asked it a different way. I said, "So, you want to stay here with us?" And, again, his head moved, ever so slightly, up and down and I exclaimed, "Then, that's how we're going to continue praying!" You see, he was still hanging between life and death and I didn't know if he would become a vegetable and would, possibly, resent the helpless life that that presents. However, if he wanted to stay with us then we definitely wanted him to stay with us and we would do everything in our power to help him to become strong again. Of course, by the help and grace of the Lord!

Chapter 16

sine qua non

THE POWER OF PRAYER

I was concerned, still, that by holding my husband's life through prayer and intercession that he would be left to live like a vegetable. I knew that this would hard for him to accept. I realized that at some point, it could come to my being asked to make the decision, whether or not, to take him off of life-support. I was remembering his and my most recent discussion about this—just that past August when my dear adjutant, Missionary Sarah Croyle, at age forty-four, had passed away of pancreatic cancer. My husband and I had reiterated to one another that, if it ever came to a decision such as that, we should not be left to linger on life support. I asked for counsel from a nurse counselor staff at the hospital. God was so faithful to me at every turn of events and gave the right person who would give me right counsel. She said, "You really don't have to make a decision in this—the fact that he has made it so far in the face of everything that has happened says to me that God is in control!" I was so relieved and thanked her, profusely, for helping me to understand this moment of indecision. God was in control and always faithful. Just trust Him to bring us through to an expected end out of this situation! Expect that my husband would fully recover no matter how dire everything looked at the time. Expect God to move in our behalf even though one physician told me that he could be hospitalized for six months. Expect God!

There are so many crisis and challenges that happened during this time. I'm just remembering the retired physician that is a part of the men's coffee group that my husband belongs to. His son was one of the cardiac specialists assigned to my husband's case. A Saturday evening, a pretty sizable group of friends and family were camped out in the Davies Family Waiting Room and I was lying on a sofa trying to rest a little. I was pretty tired most of the time those days—both emotionally and physically. Anyway, I opened my eyes briefly to see this retired physician approaching and he insisted on not only waking me up but with his loud voice attracted the attention of everyone anywhere near our group. He was arguing with me about when my husband sustained those burns and the seriousness of them. I didn't want wrong information shouted out because it could've been overheard by a newspaper person or others interested for the wrong reasons. Actually, I had to stand this man to the face and almost shout him down to get him to stop—he was so convinced that he knew exactly what had happened and what was going on with our situation and he was dead wrong. This left a bad taste in my spirit for this person that lasted a long time. There was another confrontation later by this same gentleman that I'll discuss further on. It just seemed that I was not only having to fight for my husband's life, rights, safety, spiritual well-being and respect but it just seemed like an all out fight every place I turned. Regardless, I was determined to do everything in my power and beyond (the Lord) in order that we would come out of this situation in a good way. I knew that God would see us through every obstacle. Expect God! I did! I do!

During this time, our family members were traveling back and forth from Minneapolis to Rapid City every few days and it was so wonderful to be able to lean upon our sons Thomas, Scott and Loren. However, it was Scott who assumed the role of second in command as far as speaking with the physicians, nurses and other medical staff. He also had to help me develop and monitor the visitation situation since my husband was in such a dire condition. The length of visits and number of people allowed to go into his intensive care room was so very limited until we had to establish a list of permitted visitors and length of visitation times. There were times that he had to handle things long distance from Minneapolis but he was both responsible and dependable and a shoulder for me to lean upon. Leona Derden took her role as "sister" so seriously until she would spend her own money to fly back and forth from Minneapolis; pay for a hotel near the hospital; and would spend nights in his room caring for her "dad". This was truly a time of love, support and nurturing for me.

At one point, however, I thought that I should begin to prepare our sons for the worse—just in case. As I began to try to approach that conversation with our youngest son, Loren, he was not having it! He just said, "Mom, I don't care what it looks like, my dad is going to come out of this and he is going to be just fine!" One day, it didn't look so good and Loren wasn't able to look at his father without bursting into heartbreaking tears. Even with those hot tears streaming down his face he still, stubbornly, clung to the fact that "MY DAD IS COMING OUT OF THIS!" He was torn and weeping but he wasn't taking any other answer except that his father was going to be all right.

Chapter 17

SEMBLANCE OF RETURN

His first attempts to learn speak and to write again. He communicated with us, mostly through nods, grunts and pointing. He would make direct eye contact with us and try to say whatever it was he wanted to say but words weren't coming forth yet. There were a few times that Thomas and Scott, on separate occasions, thought that he was trying to get them to help him to escape from the hospital bed. I don't blame him, after all, he was strapped down and almost bolted down in every way that he could be. His swollen hands were strapped to clothe wrapped boards. His burnt raw legs were both wrapped and strapped so that he would not move about too much and cause more damage. He could not be turned, in the bed, so they stood the bed on end and strapped him in an upright position with his feet resting on the bed's footboard. One day, through his eye movements and insinuations he had just about convinced Thomas to remove all those tubes and dash him down the hall and out of that hospital. Thomas, our eldest son, so badly wanted to comply with his dad's wishes and knew that he could not until he just burst into tears and went barreling out of that room and down the hall. Can you imagine this big, six-foot-four-inch and more than three-hundred-pound son of ours? He was heartbroken that he could do not do anything to help his dad—especially to help him escape from all that torture that he was going through. He said, "Dad! I can't! If I do, Dad, you won't be able to live . . . Dad! I can't!" As big as he was, Thomas was such a gentle giant and watching his father go through this just about killed him right there.

Early on in this whole process, along with the daily telephone briefing, the Lord gave me another idea as to how the visitors could let their voices be heard. Oh the visitors poured into the hospital day and night bringing prayers, meals, their heartfelt concerns, and all. There was no way that my husband could receive these wonderful visitors so I placed a loose leaf binder in the waiting room area where we gathered. Those who wanted to write their heartfelt thoughts were encouraged to leave their messages in this notebook so that, when he was well, he would be able to experience their visit in written form. Oh, there were so many floral arrangements and get well cards sent and/or brought but, the flowers in particular, could not be placed in his room because of all the risks of infections. Instead, since most of our hours were spent at the hospital, we just placed them around the waiting room. We strung a beautiful cord and taped all the cards on it and draped it around the waiting room where possible. We never had to go out for meals—somehow, people just seemed to know exactly what to bring and what we needed. More than enough in every instance and I was again thankful for the goodness of the Lord. He used so many different people to bring us wonderful blessings throughout those dark days. God is so good!

His birthday, February 18. It was on our annual calendar that Bishop Kelly would present a concert which would be held on Friday, February 17, in celebration of his sixty-third birthday. Our sons and I decided that we would hold the concert, anyway, and that we would do the singing. By this time, my husband's youngest sister, Neva Brown, had arrived and she ministers in liturgical dance so she was also on the program. It was like pulling teeth to convince our god daughter, Mae Hoffman, to also take part but WHEN SHE OPENED HER MOUTH TO SING we just wanted to shout in the spirit. It was a good evening—a wonderful program, we were just missing the star of the show. We were now close to three weeks since he fell ill and we were starting to see signs of improvement, slowly. Faith was to have its perfect work! Hope was beginning to take root. Ahhh! God was, indeed, working for us!

Chapter 18

Dieu defend le droit

HE SHALL LIVE AND NOT DIE!

I think it was about this time that I had visited him on Sunday morning before going to worship service at church. He was just starting to write and he wrote a note that said, "I saw our moms!" I didn't know if this was one of those visits where the previously deceased visits the person who is dying, or not. I answered him slowly and thoughtfully, and said, "You did? What did they look like and what were they doing?" He answered by motioning with his upraised hands and moving the hands wide apart from each other. He softly laughed. I said, "Oh, they were still wide?" He shook his affirmatively and smiled with glee. I could tell that he was so happy to have seen them and they were not coming after him since he had been where they were and had returned. Thank God! At church that morning, I told them how he was doing and that he had seen our moms. Then, I laughingly advised the congregation that, "If you want to be skinny in heaven then you'd better work on it down here." They laughed, of course. It was much later when Lorenzo was able to tell us more about his visit to heaven and that he had seen the hot flames of fire shooting up, out of the ground, and that a man in the distance waved him away from the fires of hell. It was right after that that he saw our moms, standing together, and he said that they were doing their most favorite thing . . . eating! Also, they both were working with aborted babies who had returned to heaven. You will read more about his experience in his portion of the book.

On that Sunday afternoon, the day after his birthday, our children were preparing to leave again to return to Minneapolis. They had been coming back and forth during the past three weeks. After church, they all came to kiss him and spend time in his room. The nurses even allowed our granddaughters to come in, into the surgical intensive care ward for a brief visit. After their farewells, I decided to play the video from the concert that we had just done for his birthday. He couldn't see yet and couldn't really speak but I still thought he would enjoy hearing our sons and all of us singing instead of him. I said, "We did it for you, honey!" and he just nodded his head. Pretty soon, a nurse arrived with a dialysis unit and said that they needed to run a dialysis on him again. He had been continuing to get dialysis several times a week in order to remove the excess fluids from his body. Surgeries related to the dialysis were frequent because they had to find new locations for the pic line—the veins that they were using would close and they'd have to find a new spot. They used his arms, his chest, his groin and his shoulder. While he was on the dialysis machine on this particular day, he wrote and note and asked, "Is that Joy?" "Joy?" I didn't know what he meant or what he was trying to ask me. Later on, I understood that this was the same dialysis nurse that served his mom while she was a dialysis patient more than fourteen years before. He was alert. He recognized her and just wanted to make sure that it was who he thought she was.

By this time, our kids were at the house packing up to get back on the road. Of course, a number of people were in the waiting room as a show of continual support. Neva and I were in the room and we still had the video going of the concert service. He had been on dialysis for, maybe an hour or more, when he began to make circular motions just above his chest and he stretched his eyes and looked at me. As he tells it, he had coded previously while on a dialysis treatment so he knew what was happening again and that's why he was making those motions. He was trying to let me know what was happening. I said to the nurse, "What's happening?" She jumped into action and began to, what looked like panic to me, exclaim . . . "Oh, Sir! I'm sorry! I took too much off! I'm sorry, SIR!" She was literally running in circles and she grabbed a pint sized container and continued to exclaim . . . "I'm going to put some back, SIR!" I ran out to the desk and asked for his main nurse and told her that there was some serious problems happening and she hastily came into his room. By now his blood pressure was rapidly dropping . . . I remember that the bottom number was at about 26, and I don't remember what the top number was but it was small. The nurses at the desk were on the telephone trying to find the doctor. It was a Sunday and there wasn't a physician there right at the time. I began to read scripture to him including Psalm 118, "I shall live and not die, to declare the . . ." I was also praying over him and calling him back. He had that far-off stare and his face was blank, and I began to say to him, "Loren! Don't you leave! You COME BACK IN THE NAME OF JESUS!" I would then declare more Scripture into him. In the meantime, his sister Neva was I MEAN fighting Satan. I heard her say, as she would walk from the side to the bottom of the bed and back, "NO YOU DON'T, SATAN!" Then she would break off into an unknown tongue that was powerful enough to send the Devil scooting and running! Between the two of us, there was some spiritual warfare going on right there! This whole episode had started around four o'clock that afternoon and I had managed to get a phone call in to the children and to ask them not to leave town but to get back over to the hospital. Around six o'clock, I got a phone call in to the church and when Elder Stephen Zieg answered the phone and, hurriedly, explained to him what was happening and that we needed prayer covering immediately. I was so concerned about the dropping blood pressure and when I mentioned that to one of the nurses, she said, "We're more concerned about the Atrial Fribrilation. He's in Atrial Fribilation and we need the doctor to tell us which medicine to use to bring him out of it. By now, doctors started arriving and they made us leave the room so they could do what they could do. Our work was done, anyway! THAT WAS SOMETHING! After seeing that their dad was going to be okay, our children left for Minneapolis the next morning. God is so good!

Chapter 19

coûte que coûte

DECLARATION . . . NO MORE DIALYSIS!

The next day, I asked the nurses and the doctors to perform NO procedures on my husband, today! "Let's let him have a day of rest!" They complied and later on that day they called me about permission to do something and I reminded them to "Do nothing today, just let him rest!" Now, mind you, my husband had been trying to write for a couple of weeks but, when we would hold the paper and clipboard up for him, his writing would slide into a diagonal line with a couple of loops. He would always look at us to see if we understood what he was trying to say and we didn't because we couldn't understand the scribbling. On this particular day, however, the day after the dialysis fiasco, he wrote. The letters were sideways and some were upside down but we understood what he was saying. I've kept that piece of paper—it's priceless! His words, though incorrectly spelled, were very understandable and they said, "N-O-O-O-O-O D-I-A-L-Y-Z." He wrote it twice and both times it was upside down or sideways on that paper—the letters were large and we all, finally, understood what he was saying. I turned to the nurse and repeated his request. Pretty soon, one doctor and then another showed up who had been summoned from home by the nurse's station. Dr. Gordon asked me to step out of the room and to speak with him in the hallway and I did. He said to me, "Mrs. Kelly. Does your husband understand what he is saying?" I said, "I'm sure he does. His mother was a dialysis patient for seven years before her passing so he knows what dialysis is . . . and he knows that he is refusing to have it done on him again!" I'll never forget that doctor's face. He was astonished as he exclaimed to me, "But, MRS. KELLY, without dialysis, he will die!" I gave some thought to what he said before I answered him, again. Then, I said, "I understand what you're saying, Dr. Gordon, but my husband says 'no more dialysis' so, there will be no more dialysis performed on him!"

Three nights later, Dr. Gordon stopped by the room again while I was there and asked me to step out into the hallway. He explained again the severity of the decision of no more dialysis and that in a split second, "Your husband could die! In the middle of the night, suddenly!" He continued and said, "I'm going to ask you to sign a paper saying that you understand this and that you stand by this decision." I said, "Okay!" and I signed the paper. Well, I'm thinking that was truly our turn around since it was another day or two that my husband was promoted from the surgical intensive care ward to the second floor's medical intensive care ward. He was moved on the following Sunday afternoon—we still had to gown up to visit him as he was still carrying the infection as well as needing to be protected from our germs. This was a happy day (twenty three days after it had all began) when he was discharged from one ward to another.

Chapter 20

tant mieux

MOVEMENT—VICTORY

February 22, 2006. He was moved to the medical intensive care ward and was there for one week as his miraculous recovery continued. In this ward they predicted he'd be there for at least a couple of weeks but he declared, "Oh, no! I'm getting out of here!" As you can tell, he was talking by then. He was talking but it was with raspy short whispers—oh, but you could understand what he was saying.

We had developed an overnight schedule where someone spent the night in his hospital room with him. Usually it would be myself, Elder Carr, Attorney Al Scovel, Sister Linda Ault, Evangelist Twana Carr, Sister Leona Derden from Minneapolis, Sister Franceen Robinson or Missionary Leonne Seevers. On one particular morning, very early, Sister Leonne had spent the night and called to tell me that "Dad wants you to get here as soon as possible. They've said that they're coming to take him to dialysis and he's trying to tell them that he's not take dialysis anymore. Please hurry as soon as you can!" I DID! When I jumped off the elevator my feet were flying down that hallway as I rushed to his room. I spoke to the nurses and told them in no uncertain terms were they to force my husband to receive dialysis. They said the doctor had ordered it. I stood firm and that was the end of that!

It was around this same time that Dr. Gordon had stopped by to check in on his "miracle" patient. I heard my husband telling him that, "Dr. Gordon, I died while I was on dialysis and I was on my way back to heaven when I heard my wife's voice call me back." I don't know how much of this the doctor believed but I was surprised to hear my husband saying this because I had not had the chance to discuss that Sunday afternoon when I had, indeed, commanded him through words and through prayer not to leave me but to come back and stay. On this same subject, it was several months later while we were visiting Chicago and having a conversation with Bishop and Mrs. James Austin when Bishop Kelly brought it up again. I broke into the conversation and began to tell them about what happened that day with Neva cursing Satan and me praying, reading scripture and call him back. He looked so surprised to have his experience confirmed. It wasn't that he doubted that what he said was true. It was that I had never thought to tell him about it since he seemed to already know what had happened without my having told him about it.

February 26, 2006. He was transferred down the hall to the pulmonary care unit where they completely removed his breathing tube and helped him through the process of learning to breathe independently again. Sometime or another, we were told that his vocal cords had been damaged by the breathing tube being left in place too long. The prospects of his speaking normally again were very slim and, the projected, "Maybe in about a year the one good vocal cord that still functioning will begin to compensate for the one that is damaged. If he ever speaks normally again, it will be a while!"

Sometime, earlier that week was when they had finally removed the breathing tube and had performed the tracheotomy. Oh, he was so afraid when he would have to try to breathe without the breathing tube. In a few short seconds, he would be gasping for air and motioning that he needed it. He was still having trouble adjusting to the removal of the breathing tube and trusting himself to breathe without help. That was a frightening time for him but he continued to improve—God is so awesome!

All along since coming out of the critical stages, whenever my husband would try to see through his glasses he would just take them off, in frustration, because he could not see through them. A specialist came in to examine his eyes and it was learned that, during the time that he was frozen, because of the length of time that the blood supply did not reach his eyes, there was a big problem. They told us that he had had three strokes in the right eye and two in the left eye and that there wasn't anything that could be done. This was very discouraging to my husband and this was the first time I'd seen him get a pout going on. He'd taken everything pretty much in stride as one piece of information about his dire conditions were told to him. This time, he got mad and got a little attitude with the Lord! I'm not advising this as a way for moving God into action I'm just saying that's what happened. The morning after receiving this terrible news from the Ophthalmologist, the Lord impressed upon him to put his glasses on and he did, after arguing a little bit, and he could now see through the same glasses he'd had all along.

March 3, 2006. By now, after his short stay in the pulmonary care unit, he was miraculously able to be transferred (promoted) to the rehabilitation center. He still had so many problems and challenges but one of the first that was conquered was getting his urine flowing, again, after such a long time of functioning with the urinary tubes. "The Pee-Pee Dance" got to be famous down the halls of Rehab because I was so excited when Lorenzo was able to urinate on his own until I took off in the dance. I grabbed the arm of the head nurse and began to sing and shuffle out the beat of a tune that just came out of my head and I named it the, "Pee-Pee Dance Song!" As the nurse and I danced arm in arm down the hall toward the Nurses station, I was hollering out that crazy tune and that was such a happy occasion for all of us. I did not then nor do I now have any embarrassment about a song called "The Pee-Pee Dance!" Every accomplishment was a victory for us and told us that my honey was truly on the road to recovery.

Chapter 21

tant pis

SEEMING SETBACKS!

During Lorenzo's stay in the Rehabilitation Institute some strange and unexplainable things began to happen. On several occasions, he would have a sudden attack of some kind where he would become weak, dizzy and faint. Hot beads of sweat would pop out all over his body and he would fall into a deep sleep for two hours during which time his pillow and clothing would become soaking wet and he would have to be changed after he awoke. It happened, a few times when he was preparing to go the physical therapy and the Physical Therapist was suspicious of this and presumed that Lorenzo was purposely trying to avoid taking the necessary therapy lesson. That was the furthest thing from my Honey's mind since he truly had no control over those occurrences. However, it made him feel upset to think that he was innocently suspect and he was concerned about the suggestion that he was trying to avoid the physical therapy sessions.

Another very upsetting thing was the amount of time that he had to wait for the leg bandages to be changed. His raw and bloody legs were in constant need of care and carefulness, however, some of the wound care team staff seemed to be unmindful about it. There was a plan in place wherein Lorenzo would receive a pain shot just before the scheduled visit but the doctor, who had to oversee the bandage changes, was usually late. By the time he would arrive the pain medication would have long worn off. The nurse would just rip the old bandage off and with it would be bunches of hairs yanked off also, often, causing my husband to scream out in pain.

After such an incident early one morning I came into his room just after having a meeting with the staff social worker about his current condition and future plans for care. As I walked through the door of his Rehab Room, he looked up at me and with great anguish he said, "I told the Lord to KILL ME OR HEAL ME! I will not live like this so He's got to do something for me! KILL ME OR HEAL ME, LORD!" he exclaimed. I just stood there looking down at him and feeling so badly that I could do

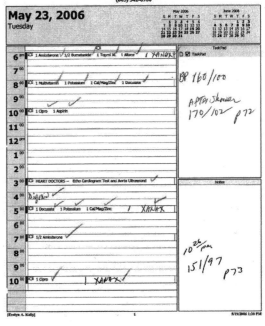

nothing to change his situation. This one was definitely on the Lord. He proved to us that HE *CAN* DO IT! He healed my husband!

In Rehab, we had continued the practice of having friends or family members sitting with Lorenzo at all times, day and night. On a particular afternoon, he called me and he said, "I've had a vision of a black cat prowling the hallway. Satan is planning another attack on me. I need you or Elder Carr to spend the night with me tonight." I had done night duty a couple of nights already that week but I knew he was right and that it wasn't just someone spending the night with him in his room but it was spiritual warfare! Not a job for just anyone! We spent the night in prayerful warfare, sleeping and praying, and we could sense that another great battle over my husband's life had been won! When we awoke the next morning, we could feel the change, the victory! That day was a great day and was the day that things finally turned around and it wasn't long before we were planning his discharge from the Rehabilitation Hospital. PRAISE THE LORD!

AT HOME: EVELYN THE NURSE!

I was ever so astonished on the day that my husband was to be released from the Rehabilitation Institute. I was simply stunned that I was the one who was going to be the head nurse NOW. First of all, having never experienced anything like this before, I just thought someone else would be responsible for supervising his medicine intake schedule and so many other things that had been handled at the hospital. As I sat in the nurses office listening to her explain MY responsibilities I was overwhelmed and it took some moments for me to understand what my new role was going to be.

My GOD! What on earth do people do who are as ill or more than my husband who have no one there to take care of their urgent needs. I thought about my late father, Clifton, and the fact that he had had two open heart surgeries and since he lived in Illinois and I lived in South Dakota, I was not there for him when he was released from the hospital. Neither was I there to make sure that he didn't take the wrong medication at the wrong time. This is serious business!

It took me a while but eventually I came up with an organized plan and it worked out very well for us. See the diagram on the right, here and you might just be very impressed with Nurse Evelyn!

Even so, my home care challenges were not over by a long shot. After all the skin graft surgeries to his legs were done, Lorenzo had to wear extremely tight support hosiery. Not only did he have to wear them but SOMEBODY had to put them on for him since he did not have the strength to do it himself. I remember the home health-care nurse when she was the first one to try to put them on him, breaking into a great sweat by the time she was done. At that point, it hadn't dawned on me that when she was no longer coming for her daily visits that I WOULD BE the one responsible for this gigantic task. Well, the day finally came and I didn't have the strength to pull those hose up on his legs—as hard as I pulled, grunted and pulled some more I just couldn't do it. Franceen Robinson was still staying with us and she was able to get them on him. She was also the one, early on, who assisted the nurses with giving Lorenzo his wash-up baths. I was never able to pay her for what she did for us during this awful time—I'm trusting that the Lord, Himself, has taken care of and is taken care of her every precious need. Anyway, eventually, I was able to get them on him without all the sweating and frustration.

The other challenges came with getting Lorenzo interested in eating again. He had stopped eating while he was in the hospital and would eat just a little of the meals that I would prepare and take there for him. Now that he was at home, he often wanted to skip his meals—just had no interest. I thank God for Sister Linda Ault who came daily (first the hospital and second to the house) to sit with my husband. Sister Linda would threaten to "Tell Sister Kelly" if he decided not to eat while I was away at work. As I mentioned earlier, Franceen had moved in the first weekend that the aneurysm occurred and stayed with me (and then with us) for several months. She would get up early in the morning and do whatever she could then go to work and return afterward to do whatever was needed. Sometimes the leg wounds would bleed through the bandages and it was "Froby," as I call her, who would be there to change the bandages for us. She was so skilled at all of those things because she works at the hospital as a nurse's aide. What a blessing that was for us. Just thinking about those two ladies, good friends they are, Froby and Linda, I am yet THANKING the Lord for having them there for us. God could never bless them too much for their kindnesses toward us during such a devastating and tremendous time!

There is so much more to this story of God's resurrection power for my husband's life. This book is an attempt to share some of the main challenges and victories that the Lord brought us through. I'm reminded of President Obama's campaign slogan of "Yes, I can!" Well, our LORD is greater than any mere human being and when we trust Him we find that "YES, HE CAN!" He can do anything but fail.

Chapter 22

THE DIVINE SEAL

It is just over four years since everything happened and we are in the 2009 Christmas season. After our morning worship service, two days past the wonderful celebration of the birth of Jesus Christ, Elder Larry Davis wanted to take some pictures of my husband and me. I asked Brother Joe to get my camera so that I could have a current photo also, after we snapped pictures with each of the camera's, we were amazed to see the "Divine Seal," resting on the left shoulder of my husband's suit and just above his left shoulder. We gasped!

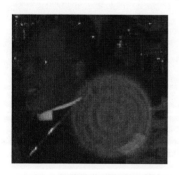

This phenomenon was continuing. At first, it seemed that it was only showing up through Sister Franceen Robinson's camera. Later on, it showed up in the picture taken with one of my three cameras. On this particular day, however, the "seal" showed up both in the pictures taken with a different one of my cameras as well as in those taken with Elder Davis's camera. The emblem shows up in pictures above, around or on my husband and usually when he is testifying about seeing heaven and hell and the time he spent with the Lord. He had just shared it, again, in his sermon that morning—the last Sunday in 2009.

Lord is trying to tell us something magnificent about this miraculous man of God and I am trying to understand just what it is that the Lord would have us to know. Why is the Lord placing this object in pictures taken of my husband? What is the meaning and message of it??

I went online and looked up the "Divine Seal and Capstone Signature of God's Word" and found some information. This symbol is known by

several names and one is a Sevenfold Symmetric Designed on the Union of Four Biblical Symbols. And he that sat upon the throne said, **Behold, I make all things new.** And he said unto me, Write: for these words are true and faithful. And he said unto me, **"It is done. I am Alpha and Omega, the beginning and the end. I will give unto him that is athirst of the fountain of the water of life** freely. **He that overcometh shall inherit all things; and I will be his God, and he shall be my son"**—Revelation.21:5

AN OVERCOMER

One thing that we can all testify to is the fact that Bishop Lorenzo L. Kelly has indeed overcome the power of death. With strength that I'm sure he would not have imagined to have had, he has become a symbol of God's power and possibility in all of our lives today! May God forever be glorified because of His great and wonderful work in the midst of death—there is life!

The Appendix

FOREIGN WORDS AND PHRASES USED IN THE CHAPTER HEADINGS

PRELUDE	in medias res (L)	In the middle of a sequence of events
Chapter 1	annus mirabiis (L)	A year of wonders or disasters
Chapter 2	in extremis (L)	At the point of death
Chapter 3	pro tempore (L)	For the time being; temporarily
Chapter 4	pleno jure (L)	With full authority
Chapter 5	sans peur et sans reproche (F)	Without fear and without reproach
Chapter 6	mirabilia (L)	Miracles
Chapter 7	omnia vincit amor (L)	Love conquers all
Chapter 8	gaudeamus igitur (L	Let us then be joyful
Chapter 9	laus Deo (L)	Praise be to God
Chapter 10	sans souci (F)	Carefree
Chapter 11	nolens volens (L)	Whether willing or not
Chapter 12	locus in quo (L)	The place in which
Chapter 13	in extremis (L)	At the point of death
Chapter 14	suo jure (L)	In ones own right
Chapter 15	in medias res (L)	In the middle of a sequence of events
Chapter 16	sine qua non (L)	Something essential
Chapter 17	ecce homo (L)	Behold the man
Chapter 18	Dieu defend le droit (F)	God defends the right
Chapter 19	coûte que coûte (F)	Cost what it may
Chapter 20	tant mieux (F)	So much the better
Chapter 21	tant pis (F)	So much the worse
Chapter 22	integer vitae scelerisque (L)	Upright in life and free from wickedness

VARIOUS STAGES OF THE LEG BURNS, GRAFTS AND DONOR SITES. AFTER ALL THAT, IT WAS SO GOOD TO BE WALKING AGAIN!

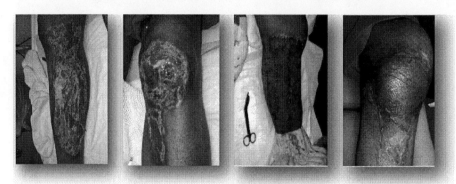

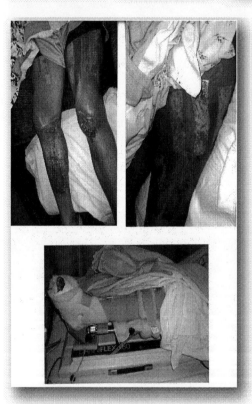

At first they were thought to be 2nd degree burns but later it was learned they were 4th. Muscle from my legs and skin from my hips and thighs was used to cover the wounds.

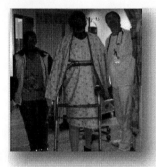

**SOME OF THE
MEDICAL
INTENSIVE CARE
NURSES WHO
WERE SO KIND**

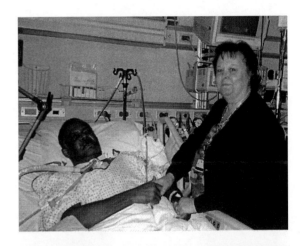

EVENTS THAT HAPPENED WITHIN THE MONTH PRECEDING THE ANEURYSM

Students, bishop celebrate MLK

←He spoke
At Stevens High School on Friday, January 13, 2006

He hosted →
the annual Martin Luther King Jr. Birthday Memorial Service on Monday, January 16, 2006,

at Faith Temple Church in Rapid City, South Dakota

MLK: Importance of the holiday

His fourth granddaughter Beatriz was born in Minneapolis on January 8.

He visited
and held in his arms Isaac Taylor, our newborn god grand baby born at Rapid City Regional Hospital on January 16, 2006. →

He traveled
to Jonesboro, Arkansas, and preached revival services on January 17 through 22 and returned home on Tuesday, January 24, 2006. He carried on normal routine at the office and visited Pennington County Jail inmates during the week. Then had a wonderful evening with his wife on Friday, January 27. No one would look at this healthy-looking man of God and suspect what was just around the corner for his life!

#1

#2

#3

MEDICAL RECORDS EXCERPTS

HISTORY OF PRESENT ILLNESS

The patient is a pleasant sixty-two-year-old African-American, well-developed and well-nourished male. A local minister who was presented to the hospital on January 28, 2006 with sudden onset of severe midsternal chest pain radiating to the back and abdomen described as throbbing pain. He was found to have a type-A dissection by CT scan. He had a previous history of a small aortic aneurysm. The dissection extends all the way down the thoracic aorta down to the level of the renal origins. He was taken emergently to surgery by Dr. Gordon and underwent the following: (1) replacement of the ascending aorta, (2) resuspension of the aortic valve leaflets, (3) replacement of the transverse arch, (4) reim—plantation of the innominate artery, left carotid and left subclavian arteries, as well as (5) replacement of the upper descending thoracic aorta.

The patient's postoperative course: The patient had some renal issues, which required temporary dialysis, which was subsequently resolved. The patient also had multiple episodes of atrial fibrillation, which he did not tolerate. He had to be shocked numerous times in order to resolve the atrial fibrillation. Additionally during the procedure, while warming, he was using a pediatric warmer on the legs. Apparently, the patient had developed some burns, which at the time did not appear to be significant, but later turned into fourth-degree burns on both legs. There were a number of consults in this case including renal, pulmonary, cardiology, and plastic surgery. Dr. Schutz was consulted in the future plans to do skin grafts. The patient has done well after emergency repair of acute dissection of the ascending aorta arch and descending thoracic aorta and is being discharged to followup care by Dr. Gordon, Dr. Schabauer, and Dr. Schutz.

March 3, 2006 Discharge Summary

He has bilaterial burns to his medial knees and medial upper lower extremities.

He was returned to the operating room for reexploration for bleeding on January 29, 2006.

During surgery and following surgery, he has received massive blood transfusions. He received thirty-seven units of packed cells plus other blood products.

His chest or sternum was left open postoperatively. Patient is intubated orally. He has a right radial arterial line. He has a Swan-Ganz catheter from the right internal jugular. He has a dialysis catheter via the left femoral vein. The patient had atrial fibrillation with rapid ventricular response post closure of the sternum. His blood pressure did not tolerate the high heart rate. Because of the above factors, it will be important to try to maintain sinus rhythm.

He is on a ventilator and sedated. He is being ventilated with tidal volumes of 800. With this, he has peak airway pressures of 26 to 28, high flow pressures of 19 to 21. His compliance is 56. He is currently on 40 percent oxygen, SIMV with a rate of 12, tidal volume of 800 mL. He is not on CRRT for fluid overload. He is making urine. He is on propofol for sedation. He had been taking Levaquin before hospitalization for an upper respiratory tract infection.

He was subsequently taken back to surgery on the January 31, 2006, for closure of the sternum. He tolerated the procedure well and was returned to the surgical intensive care unit. He subsequently went into atrial fibrillation with rapid ventricular response up to 180 to 190 bpm associated with hemodynamic collapse. He did undergo cardioversion and was subsequently started on amiodarone IV. Dr. Teixeira, who was in the hospital at a meeting, was urgently summoned or arrhythmia management. Please see code sheet for further details. The patient was cardioverted numerous times and was given a 1-mg ibutilide infusion over ten minutes and did convert to sinus rhythm. He subsequently went into a juncrional rhythm. His amidarone was stopped. He later resumed sinus rhythm and the amiodarone infusion was continued at 0.5 mg per minute. He ventilated on Levophed and amiodarone infusions. He has four chest tubes in place. He is receiving T4 renal fusion; a Bumex drip has recently been discontinued.

Postoperative Diagnoses: Acute renal failure and respiratory failure in part due to tachyarrhythmias and shock, also retained clots with ateletasis of both upper lobes. This gentleman returned this afternoon from having his chest closed. Initially, he was doing well, and then all of a sudden, he went into V-tech. It was very difficult to control the rhythms. With this, he also developed profound hyposemia. Chest X-ray had been done and this showed atelectasis of both upper lobes. The nurses have been suctioning significant blood clots this afternoon. For this reason, emergency bronchoscopy is being performed to try to clear his airway and improve his oxygenation. This is an emergency situation, with no time to obtained informed consent. The patient is on a ventilator, 100 percent oxygen. While Dr. Gordon and Dr. Teixeira were dealing with his arrhythmias, I proceeded to perform emergency bronchoscopy. This was done with no sedation. The Olympus bronchoscope was passed via the endotracheal tube. The end of the endotracheal tube is in good position in the trachea. He had significant clots in the lower trachea that were cleared. I then went down into both left main stem and right main stem, and into both upper lobes. He had significant clots in both upper lobes that I cleared with aggressive suctioning and instilling sterile saline to remove more clots. By the end of this procedure, the airways to the upper lobes are patent. (January 31, 2006)

Mr. Kelly went into atrial fibrillation, rapid ventricular response, up to 180 bpm. He became hypotensive, and 1 mg ibutilide was given IV over ten minutes with no success. A 200-joule biphasic shock was delivered, converting the patient to regular sinus rhythm. His blood pressure immediately bounced back to 110 systolic. (February 4, 2006)

Under IV sedation, a 100-joule biphasic shock was delivered after IV ibutilide, converting to regular sinus rhythm. The patient tolerated the procedure well without complications. (February 6, 2006)

Burns to lower extemity intraoperative. The patient is a sixty-three-year-old male who has suffered third- and fourth-degree burns to his bilateral lower extremities. Complicated open wounds to bilateral lower extremities. He requires debridement and closure of bilateral lower leg wounds with right soleus and left gastrocnemius muscle flaps and split-thickness skin graft coverage. Patient was admitted on March 31, 2006. He was taken to the operating room and underwent debridement of bilateral lower extremities with bilateral lower extremity muscle flap coverage and skin-graft coverage. Patient was admitted postoperatively for care and monitoring of his flaps and grafts. He continued to do well. His activity was advanced. His grafts remained stable, and he was discharged to go home on April 8, 2006, in stable condition. (April 8, 2006)

The Epilogue

My name is Loren Kelly and I am the youngest son of Bishop Lorenzo Kelly. A seed of anger started inside of me when my dad had his aneurysm just over four years ago—My daughter Beariz had been born just twenty days earlier. My dad died several times on the operating table and they kept bringing him back. When they did the surgery, they froze his body. When they were bringing him back, his legs were severely burned to the point where he might not walk again. I was angry having to watch him in so much pain and he hadn't even seen my daughter yet. He did not look like the same person laying in that bed. I watched my oldest brother scream in the hallway "No, it was supposed to be me first!" I put my face on and tried to keep it together for the family and be the strong one. Inside I was saying, "God, he was faithful to you. I have never seen him do anything contrary to your Word. How could you let something like this happen to this man of God when all he has ever done is serve you?" I was glad and thankful that my dad was ALIVE but every time I looked at his legs, I'd leave the room and break down and get angry inside. I just couldn't understand why. This was in 2006, I questioned God but I still tried to go to church and go through the motions. After awhile, my dad started recovering and things seemed like they were getting back to normal. But in the back of my head, I was thinking "Is this the fate that awaits me for serving You too?" My dad would try to keep a positive face around us but he was in depression and would randomly break down and cry. Watching this was just killing me inside.

Almost exactly two years after my dad's illness, my oldest brother Thomas had a brain aneurysm and passed away three and a half weeks later. My mom asked me to sing Amazing Grace at the funeral and I really didn't want to sing it because I wasn't feeling too much grace at that moment. I sang from a place of pain that I've never felt and I almost didn't make it through. Then I watched my dad preach one of the most open, powerful, real sermons he has ever preached. At the funeral there were maybe 400 or 500 people that came -- some I hadn't seen for years. My dad was preaching the sermon of his life and so many people were touched so much that this was a life changing event for them. However the seed of anger just embedded itself a little deeper inside of me.

It has now been over two years since my brother died and I have lived in what seemed like pure hell. I allowed myself to put many things in my life in order to soothe the pain of loss and grief. Recently my eyes have come open and I can see that I was in the very clutches of Satan. I have repented to the Lord and am now in grief and life recovery. Also, and most importantly, I have just renewed my relationship with the Lord. Now I can finally say that the Lord is good and His mercy is everlasting. His truth endures to all generations! You may not always understand why God allows things to happen in your life but as you continue in life and in relationship with the Lord you will receive the grace and strength to go through whatever situation God allows.

I've seen this in my dad. Now I have this gift for myself also.

Get Published, Inc!
Thorofare, NJ 08086
02 April, 2010
BA2010092